Machiavellian
POKER STRATEGY

LYLE STUART

Kensington Publishing Corp.
www.kensingtonbooks.com

Machiavellian
POKER STRATEGY

*How to Play Like a Prince
and Rule the Poker Table*

DAVID APOSTOLICO

LYLE STUART BOOKS are published by

Kensington Publishing Corp.
850 Third Avenue
New York, NY 10022

All Kensington titles, imprints, and distributed lines are available at special quantity discounts for bulk purchases for sales promotions, premiums, fund-raising, educational, or institutional use. Special book excerpts or customized printings can also be created to fit specific needs. For details, write or phone the office of the Kensington special sales manager: Kensington Publishing Corp., 850 Third Avenue, New York, NY 10022, attn: Special Sales Department; phone 1-800-221-2647.

Lyle Stuart is a trademark of Kensington Publishing Corp.

First printing: September 2005

10   9   8   7   6   5   4   3   2   1

Printed in the United States of America

ISBN 0-8184-0651-8

To Cindy, you're the best!

Contents

Introduction

Mention Machiavelli and five words immediately come to mind: the end justifies the means. Throughout the centuries since Machiavelli first penned *The Prince*, countless people in various cultures and walks of life have interpreted and analyzed his work. Many have used his advice to rationalize their ruthless behavior.

In truth, Machiavelli never intended that his advice for a Prince serve as a justification for a complete abandonment of morality. Machiavelli did struggle with questions of morality and ethics, but he believed that questionable behavior on the part of leaders would be forgiven or ignored if the people benefited. Machiavelli was also a pragmatist. He advised that leaders may have to commit some untoward acts to both gain and retain positions of power.

Machiavelli's views of human nature were revolutionary for their time. He believed that man could control his own destiny or at least have a say in it. At the time, the common wisdom was that everything that took place on Earth was predetermined. While Machiavelli recognized that Fortune (the Roman goddess of Luck) did in fact play a large part in everything that transpired in life, he believed that man could also change his course in life. Machiavelli went as far as to say that Fortune was responsible for one half of man's destiny while man controlled the other half. In addition, if a man were to be proactive, he could prepare for the ill effects of Fortune and greatly diminish her impact.

Machiavelli believed in the individual's ability to achieve great things and take control of his own life. A man's private morality is to be completely separate from his public life. What makes one a good person is different from what makes one an effective and successful leader. What if one could find the perfect arena to apply Machiavelli's lessons? A place where one is greatly rewarded for taking control of his opponents? A place where one does not have to struggle with questions of morality or ethics? A place where Fortune plays a tremendous role and one needs to know how to deal with her effects?

Such a place exists. It is called the poker room, and it is the perfect laboratory to apply Machiavelli's teachings. (Note: While poker is a gender-neutral game, for simplicity's sake I have used the masculine third person where I could have just as easily used the feminine. It is meant to be neutral.)

I.
Si guarda al fine

"In the actions of all men, and especially of princes, where there is no court of appeals, one judges by the result." *Si guarda al fine*: one judges by the result. This is perhaps Machiavelli's most famous, and most misunderstood, passage. It has often been interpreted to imply that the end justifies the means. In other words, one can use whatever means necessary, no matter how evil, so long as it leads to a greater good in the end. However, it is not certain that Machiavelli advocated the total elimination of morality from the means.

What is certain is that Machiavelli wrote about what political power is and how to both obtain and keep it. He was a realist about human nature and the characteristics people looked for in a leader. He recognized that the people will largely ignore the means (even if immoral) a leader employs to achieve an end that benefits the people. He also recognized that those seeking political power would do almost anything to both obtain and keep it. Again, if the people benefited from one's leadership, they were apt to ignore the means employed to gain and keep such power.

In poker, there are no moral dilemmas. There is no court of appeals. One needs only to look at the result, and there is no contest in which it is easier to keep score than poker. You are either up or down, winning money or losing money. Everyone has the same goal, and every player is not only allowed but expected, to use all means necessary to accomplish that end.

There are no moral dilemmas.

You have only one goal in poker and that is to win money. Even if you are purely a recreational player, you are playing in order to compete. You owe it to yourself and your opponents to play with all due earnestness in order to create a true competition. While most players understand that deception is a fundamental part of the game, they fail to adopt the mind-set necessary in order to be successful. One must possess the cunning and ruthlessness that the most cynical interpretation of Machiavelli implies one must have in order to gain and keep power. The poker table is one of the few arenas in life where you can be the Prince that Machiavelli advises. This is poker. It is not war. Countries will not rise and fall with your play. World peace does not hang in the balance. Lives are not at stake. For the great majority of recreational players, the only thing dependent on a four-hour Saturday afternoon poker session is where you will eat for dinner that night. Win and you treat yourself to one of the nicer restaurants in the casino. Lose and see whether you can finagle a coupon to the $5.99 buffet. So have fun with it. Whether you are a recreational player looking for a nice meal or a professional in a high-stakes game, employ every means necessary in order to win.

Every player at the table knows the nature of the game when he sits down. There are no favors. There is no quid pro quo. Your goal is the same as everyone else's at the table—to win money. They will be trying to take your money, so you better be prepared to defend your stack as well as attack theirs. The money you do not lose is as important as the money you win. Adopt the mind-set of a powerful leader, and view the other players at the table as your subjects. Tax them and manipulate them. Control their play and you control the table.

So how do you take advantage of your newfound lack of morality to succeed at the poker table? First, never be sympathetic to your opponent. Your goal is not only to win money but to win the maximum amount of money possible. Do not give your opponents free, or cheap, cards when they are chasing *runners* that could beat you. When your opponent is *drawing dead* against your winning hand, do everything possible to keep him in the hand to maximize your profit. For example, say you are playing

$1–$5 seven card stud where you can *bet* anywhere from $1 to $5. On *fifth street*, your hand looks like this:

K♠ 3♣   3♠ K♦ K♣
hole cards   turned over

There are two other players in the *pot*, and neither one has an ace showing or a *pair* on the *board*. Both players are *loose*, and you believe one player is chasing a *flush* and the other a *straight*. In any event, you know you are an overwhelming *favorite* to win the hand. At this point, your goal is to play the hand to maximum profit. The pot currently has $10. Since you are the first to act, you must bet that amount which will maximize your return. Given that your hand is not completely hidden, you should not *check*. To do so would tip off your opponents that you possess a monster hand. Conversely, you should not bet $5, as that is likely to *chase* even these loose opponents away. So you should bet that amount which both these players are likely to *call*. Because you did not pair your door card, a $2 or $3 bet may be interpreted that you have only a pair of Kings. If you believe only one player would call a $3 bet but both players would call a $2 bet, then bet $2. Not only will you make an extra dollar on this round of betting, but you will now give two players the opportunity to make a hand that will be very profitable to you. Since your opponents are unlikely to put you on a *full house*, if they hit their straight or draw, you will be paid off.

While you should never be sympathetic to your opponents, you should not be unpleasant to them either. Besides being bad manners, it is poor poker as well. Say in the preceding example that you know both of your opponents are extremely loose and will call just about any bet no matter what they are holding. So instead of betting $2 on fifth street, you bet $5. Sure enough, both players call. On *sixth street* you bet another $5, and again both players call. On the *river*, you bet another $5 dollars, and one player *folds* while the other player *raises* $5. Bingo. You feel confident he hit his straight, so you re-raise $5, and, to your surprise, he re-raises another $5.

Now at this point, you have no idea what to expect from this player, and even though he does not have a pair on board, you call rather than raise again. He turns over three deuces to go with the deuce he hit on sixth street giving him four of a kind to your full house. You cannot believe your misfortune. Your opponent calls a $5 bet on fifth street with nothing but a pair of deuces against your full house. Then he gets another deuce on sixth street, and the miracle deuce on the river.

You cannot believe how lucky he is and what a *bad beat* you have just taken. In your frustration, you berate your opponent to let him know how dumb he was to have played that hand, and if he had not been so incredibly lucky, he would have lost a fortune. I have seen this kind of behavior at the poker table countless times. Not only is it despicable, but it is an exercise of extremely poor judgment. You should be doing everything in your control to encourage play like that. Tell your opponent, "Nice hand" and "It sure is tough to scare you out of a pot." Let him feel good about himself and his play. If he keeps playing like that, you will more than make up for the occasional bad beat. If you berate him, he is apt to change his style of play or, even worse, leave the table.

Remember, you can only justify the means to your end if it is for the overall good. Let everyone at the table feel good about his play. Do not brag if you are up or belittle those who make mistakes. If you are winning, act like it is just the luck of the cards and that your opponent's turn will come soon enough. So long as your opponent is having a good time, he is likely to stay at the table even if he is down. If in winning you manage to antagonize everyone else at the table, they will all get up and leave, and you will be unable to accomplish your goal. On the other hand, if you create a positive environment for the benefit of all the players at the table, they are likely to stay and play whether or not they are winning or losing. It is much better to pick someone's pocket and have them thank you for it than to take their wallet and beat 'em over the head with it. While you should ignore morality, you should maintain civility.

As everyone knows, deception is an integral and expected part of poker. Poker is one of the few arenas in life in which the art of deception is not only condoned but appreciated and respected. So use it. Do not overuse it. Do not misuse it. Do not use it just to use it. Deception is a powerful tool if used properly. You must use it discriminately and judiciously. When you choose to implement it, use it ruthlessly. Most importantly, use it in situations and against opponents when it is likely to be effective.

Deception is more than just *bluffing*. It is about concealing both your strengths and weaknesses. It is about mixing up your play so that your opponents cannot get a read on you. Whenever your opponent cannot figure out your play, you gain an advantage. You are forcing your opponent to make decisions with incomplete information. The less information your opponent has, the more likely he is to make a mistake. Every time your opponent does something he should not do, you benefit.

How do you accomplish this? First, keep your play unpredictable. If you are playing hold 'em, do not always fold to a raise when you are in the *big blind*. Even if you keep getting marginal hands, opponents will notice this and exploit it to their advantage. No matter what form of poker you are playing, play a couple of marginal starting hands aggressively. Win or lose, you will project a wild image which will defy how you are really playing and which will help you win more money later on. For example, you have been playing at a $5–$10 hold 'em table for about an hour with the same players. You have been playing very *tight*, and since you have received very few playable hands, you have not seen many *flops*. You realize at this point that if you do get a strong hand, you are not likely to get any *callers* since your opponents are likely to put you on a hand because they know you have been playing tight.

Now is a good time to play a marginal hand with strength in the right situation. Your opponents are likely to put you on a strong hand offering you a couple of different ways to win. Say you are playing in *late position* with J-9 *off-suit*. The first four players fold. The player to your immediate right *limps in*. Now is an opportune time to raise. With only the *button* and the *blinds* yet to act, you are in good position. It is unlikely the player to your right has a very strong hand, or he would have raised in that position. In any event, you have a good chance to win the pot right there with your tight image. Even if you get a caller, you have a good chance to win after the flop, even if you do not hit it. So long as none of your opponents hit the flop, they are likely to fold to any bet made by you after the flop since they will be putting you on a strong hand. This is especially true if the flop brings some scary high cards that do not help your opponents.

While there is no guarantee that you will win the hand, you are at least giving yourself the opportunity to take advantage of the tight image you have earned over the last hour of play. Either way, it is a win-win situation for you. If your hand is exposed, your opponents will have a harder time figuring out your play in the future. This will pay off when the cards do come. If you win without a fight, you have stolen a pot with a marginal hand and have still preserved your conservative image, which you can capitalize on again.

Next, conceal the real value of your hand. When you have a strong hand, play it for maximum profit. Say you are playing $1–$5 seven card stud, and there are four players in the pot on sixth street. You hit a full house on sixth street, and fortunately for you, the first player to act has hit a straight. He immediately bets $5. You are tempted to raise $5 because you are quite sure that your well-hidden full house will be called by the straight.

However, there are still two players to act after you. Both of these players are chasing flushes and are getting *pot odds* to do so. If you raise the straight, these players are sure to fold, as they will believe (correctly) that they are drawing dead. Thus, by raising, you are likely to lose two bets and gain one. That is not smart poker. You should just call in this situation. Not only do you gain the two bets from the players behind you, but you offer each of them the chance to draw a flush. By concealing information, you have two players playing a hand they should have folded. If one or both hit the flush on the river, you are sure to win a few more bets.

Adapt to the situation. Do not just blindly play your cards. Know each of your opponents' playing styles so that you can stay one step ahead of them by outwitting them. You are playing your opponents, not your cards. You want to maximize your profits and minimize your losses. If your opponent has a strong but beatable hand, try to get some cheap or *free cards*. For example, say you are playing $4–$8 hold 'em, and the player *under the gun* raises. Everyone folds to you on the button. You have K♥, Q♥ and you decide to call. The blinds fold. The flop comes A♥, 9♣, 4♥. The big blind checks and the original *raiser* bets $4. Now, it is your turn to act. You are pretty sure the bettor has an ace. However, you have the nut flush draw, so you would like to see the hand through to the river.

You also know your opponent will play his ace all the way to a *show-

down no matter what. Still, if you take control of the betting, he will concede and follow your lead. So instead of calling, you raise here. Why do this? You know your opponent will only call; which he does. Therefore, while this round of betting cost you $4 more than if you had just called, you know your opponent will now, in all likelihood, check the turn card for he fears you have an ace with a higher *kicker* or possibly even aces up.

If the turn card does not bring you any help, you can check as well and see the river for free. Since the betting on the turn card increases from $4 to $8, by preventing your opponent from betting the turn, you have saved $4. (The extra $4 you raised after the flop saved you an $8 bet on the turn.) Now that you have checked the turn, your opponent is likely to bet after the river, which is exactly what you want. If you miss the river, you simply fold. If you complete your flush, you can raise and win two bets instead of one.

The raise made after the flop in the preceding situation is an example of a *semi-bluff*. You made a raise when you were pretty sure your opponent had the better hand, but you had a decent draw to an even better hand. Of course, the ultimate form of deception is a total bluff. You implement a total bluff when you know your only chance to win is to convince your opponent that you have the better hand (when in fact you do not) by making a substantial bet or raise. Your hope is that your opponent will fold and hand you the pot without a showdown. While bluffs are a powerful tool when successful, they should be implemented only on rare occasions and typically only when you are *heads-up*. First, your opponent must be vulnerable. Your opponent cannot have a strong hand, and he must have a reason for believing you have a strong hand. If you are playing seven card stud and your four up cards are not going to scare anybody, you are in no position to bluff. Next, your opponent must not suspect you of bluffing. If you have been playing tight the whole game, you are in a much better position to sell a bluff. Finally, you must be getting correct pot odds in order to make it worth your while. If there is $20 in the pot and you believe that there is a 50 percent chance your opponent will fold if you make a $5 bet, then it makes sense to go ahead and bluff.

While you should bluff only rarely, do not be afraid to make a bluff. If you are called, you still benefit. Your opponents will be more likely to call you now in the future when you have a strong hand. Do not be embarrassed about being caught bluffing. It is part of the game and can still serve to benefit you. Furthermore, there is nothing to be embarrassed about, as you do not need to justify your play to anyone. How you play is no one's business but your own. You alone should establish the means you employ to accomplish your end goal.

There is no court of appeals.

Poker can be a cruel and unjust game. Anyone who has ever played will have countless bad beat stories. There will be times when opponents suck out on you playing hands they never should have been in. There will be times when you cannot catch a hand for anything. What can you do about these situations? Absolutely nothing. There is no court of appeals. All you can do is suck it up and maintain your composure. Poker can be a streaky and lucky game. Over the long run, however, the cards will even out. The key to an overall successful poker strategy is to maintain your discipline in order to play solid poker no matter what the situation. You cannot afford to get frustrated by a bad beat. Do not let your emotions get away from you, or you will find yourself *on tilt* (that is, playing poorly and loosely). Conversely, when things are going your way, do not allow yourself to get overconfident or careless. Play your game no matter what the situation.

That does not mean that you will play the same way all the time. Quite the opposite: you should be constantly adjusting your game to changing circumstances in order to take advantage of opportunities. However, *your game* will incorporate a strategy for adapting to situations. When you lose your composure, you will be thrown off your game, and you will make mistakes. There are no mulligans in poker. Once you commit *chips* to the pot, those chips no longer belong to you. They belong to the pot. That is why it is so critical to pay close attention to everything going on at the table, including your own state of mind. If you are playing hold'em and you flop a *set* and your opponent calls two bets to hit a backdoor flush draw, take a deep breath and say "nice hand" to your opponent. If you stay on your game, you will eventually win a lot of money from opponents continuing to chase runners.

One judges by the result.

As mentioned earlier, since there is no court of appeals, one is judged by the result. You are either up or down. You either win money or lose money. The outcome is entirely up to you. Sure, there will be times when you have minor setbacks. No matter how good you are, there will be days when you lose. But if you develop the discipline and mind-set to play solid poker consistently, then over the long run you will be successful.

Since poker can be an unjust game, you must do everything in your power to ensure that you succeed. So long as you play within the rules, you can and should use every means at your disposal to beat your opponent. Poker provides a forum for you to implement guilt free the most ruthless of Machiavellian principles. It is your opportunity to be a Prince.

II

Be a Prince

Machiavelli said that "a man who wants to make a profession of goodness in everything is bound to come to ruin among so many who are not good."

The poker table is a cruel and competitive place. You must do everything in your power to succeed, and you must recognize that everyone else at the table will be doing everything in their power to make sure you do not succeed. You cannot be weak, and you cannot show weakness. You cannot be vulnerable, and you cannot appear vulnerable. Your only goal is to maximize your profits. Any behavior or feelings on your part that can interfere with that goal are inappropriate.

A poker game is your arena to unapologetically indulge your most competitive desires. In fact, anything less than an unbridled competitive effort on your part will leave you vulnerable. If you do not put forth that effort, the opponents among you surely will.

Machiavelli cautioned that a Prince must learn how not to be good and to use this knowledge when necessary. If you want to be the leader of your table, you must do everything in your power to grab and retain power. You must adopt and implement the principles Machiavelli outlines for the Prince. Machiavelli realized that there was goodness in man. He had advised that for a Prince to obtain raw unadulterated power, the Prince had to overcome that weakness. Machiavelli believed that a Prince was justified in not being good if it was politically expedient. While one can certainly argue the merits of this principle in the political arena, there is no denying its existence and appropriateness at the poker table.

If your opponent is weak, you must attack him. If your opponent appears vulnerable, you must exploit that vulnerability. If your opponent makes a mistake, punish him. Doing these things does not make you a bad person. It makes you a good poker player who your opponents will respect and admire. Everyone knows the nature of the game when they sit down at the table. So have fun with it. Enjoy the pursuit of unadulterated power. Embrace the opportunity to compete at every level with worthy adversaries.

If your opponent is weak, attack him.

The ways an opponent can be weak are as varied as the kinds of hands you can receive. It does not matter how your opponent is weak so long as you recognize it and exploit it to your advantage. Conversely, you need to be careful to make sure you are not playing weak. It is just as important to analyze your own play consistently as it is to analyze your opponents' plays.

While the ways an opponent can be weak are many and varied, there are a few obvious situations both to look for in an opponent and to avoid yourself. The first is the player who is sitting at a higher stakes table than he can afford. The reason this player is so vulnerable is not that he is playing against better competition than he can handle (which may or may not be true), but that he is playing with scared money. He is playing not to lose rather than to win, and any player who plays that way is guaranteed to lose. Whether or not you are a professional or recreational player, you should be playing stakes with which you are comfortable. If you cannot afford to lose your stake at the table, you are extremely vulnerable. Your fear of losing is sure to cloud your judgment, and it will not take long for your opponents to sense your fear. Once they do, they will attack you relentlessly and exploit your vulnerability to their full advantage.

So always choose a table with stakes well within your means. When you can afford to lose, you are playing from strength. Then you can take advantage of those opponents who are not playing from strength. Take time to periodically reevaluate the chip stacks of all your opponents and yourself. A table with comfortable limits when you first sit down may quickly become expensive if you suffer some losses. If this happens, take care to recognize it and take a break or find a lower limit table so that you are not playing with scared money.

Another common type of weak player is the *calling station*. He will call just about any bet or raise with trash hands in the hopes of improving against tough odds. When this player does not improve by the river, he will usually fold rather than face a showdown in which he will have to turn over an embarrassingly bad hand.

How do you play against a calling station? Try to get heads-up with him when you have medium to strong hands. If he is on a draw, make him pay to keep chasing. If at any point he raises, he has probably made his hand, and you should consider folding. A bluff is worthless against a calling station at this point. If he does not raise, bet all the way until you reach the river. On the river, you must gauge how strong your hand is against his likely hand. If your hand never improves, you will need to bet out. The calling station is likely to fold if he does not make a hand even if he has you beat. If you have a medium-strong hand, you should probably check. If he does not hit his draw, you most likely have him beat, and a bet will only induce him to fold and will not make you any more money. If, however, he hits his draw, then a bet here is likely to be raised, and you have cost yourself an extra bet. Finally, if you have a very strong hand, bet out in the hopes that your opponent has made something and will call you.

Be aware that a calling station will occasionally make hands and beat you. Do not let this frustrate you. Since a calling station will be playing most hands, he will be catching some hands. This is a good thing for it will encourage his play, even though he will be losing a lot of money overall. Do not let minor setbacks alter your play. You should continue to try to get heads-up with the calling station whenever you have a playable hand. In the long run, you will win a lot of money by attacking this weak opponent.

Players who play too tight, too loose, or in any other predictable manner are weak players. Look for patterns in your opponents' play to exploit while avoiding becoming predictable yourself.

Exploit your opponent's vulnerabilities.

To be a Prince, one must defeat his opponents. You must know your opponent and his play so that you can exploit his weaknesses and take advantage of his vulnerabilities. From the time you sit down, you should be analyzing all your opponents' play. Study their moves, style, and mannerisms. Know how much they are winning or losing. Know what kinds of hands they like to play. Know what kinds of attitudes they have.

Whether you are in the hand or not, you should be studying your opponents. If you are not sure how an opponent is playing, test him. If an opponent has been playing aggressively and winning pots without a showdown, challenge him the next time you have a playable hand. If he is on a *steal*, he will fold rather than face a showdown in which he has to reveal his hand to the entire table. Even if you lose the hand, you have sent a valuable message.

Observe and probe to gather information. You want as much intelligence on your opponents as possible. Stay involved in every hand whether or not you fold. Observe all the actions of your opponents. Make a few unorthodox plays to see how your opponent reacts. This serves two purposes: it helps keep your play unpredictable, and it allows you to see how your opponent reacts. For example, say you are playing $1–$5 seven card stud where the low card has to open for at least $1. You find that one opponent likes to raise $5 when he is in late position and a couple of other players have limped in for $1. You believe this opponent is bullying the table and trying to win easy pots when he knows players are willing to bet $1 but unlikely to call a $5 raise. Next time he does this, re-raise him $5 to see how he reacts.

On the other hand, if you are playing $6–$12 limit hold'em and you find that there are a lot of players limping in pre-flop but rarely do you see a raise, then try raising yourself. See if these players are playing real hands or if they are just trying to see the flop cheaply. Even though you do not win specific pots with these probing plays, you are gaining valuable information. The more intelligence you can gather, the better prepared you will be to take advantage of your opponents' vulnerabilities. In addition, by mixing up your play, you keep your opponents from getting a read on you.

Whenever a player shows his hand, take note. A weak player will play his cards, not his opponents. If he is dealt pocket Kings in hold'em, he will play them all the way to the river even if the flop brings an ace and three of the same suit (and neither of his Kings are of that suit). He will stay in the hand even if two other players are betting into him. If you find a player calling bets all the way to the river and then *mucking* his losing hand, ask to see his cards. Most card rooms will allow you to see any hand that plays to a showdown. Even if you folded pre-flop, you have the right to ask to see any mucked hands.

If a weak player is willing to bet his strong but losing hands, let him. In hold'em, let him bet his straight when he is oblivious to the fact that the board has given you a flush. This will increase your profit especially in no limit play. The more he bets, the more committed he will be when you finally raise on the river.

A good player, on the other hand, will *lay down* strong but losing hands, even though he has a lot of money invested in the pot. This player knows that the money in the pot is no longer his. It belongs to the pot. The strong player knows how to get away from a hand and cut his losses.

A weak player will get frustrated by bad beats and go on tilt in a vain effort to win his money back. A strong player will maintain his composure and not get frustrated by losing hands. The strong player is able to play well consistently whether or not he is up or down. He will not show you his hand unless forced to do so, and you will have a hard time figuring out his play.

A weak player will fail to realize the value of a marginal hand in the right position. He will fold in the face of strength even if he has you beat. Attack weak players who are easily convinced that you possess a strong hand.

If you continue to probe and observe, you will be able to distinguish the strong players from the weak. Once you can identify the weak, concentrate on exploiting their mistakes. Probe these players further so that you can determine all their vulnerabilities. If you consistently take advantage of these weak players' vulnerabilities, you can avoid the strong players unless you have a clear advantage.

It goes without saying that if you want to exploit weak players, you want to make sure you avoid being a weak player yourself. Mix up your play, remain flexible, stay in control of your emotions, play your opponents and the situation, and avoid giving your opponents opportunities to exploit your play.

If your opponent makes a mistake, punish him.

There will be times when another player makes a mistake. Those are the times you must punish him. Make him pay for the mistake. More importantly, make him pay you for the mistake. For example, say you are playing no limit hold'em and the player under the gun raises an amount equal to the big blind pre-flop. You call in late position with Q, J *suited*. Everyone else folds. The flop comes A, 10, 3 *rainbow* with one of your suits. The original raiser is first to act, and he checks. You have played with this player before and have never known him to implement a *check-raise*. Now, having raised pre-flop in *early position*, he projects a strong starting hand. You put him on an ace with a big kicker or a pair of tens or better. When the flop shows an ace, he should bet out even if he does not have an ace. If he has made a big bet, you will have no choice but to fold. However, by not betting, he has made a mistake and given you an opportunity to win the pot. You believe he does not have an ace, in which case that is the one card he does not want to see. Take advantage of his mistake. Punish him. You believe he is scared of the ace, so give him something to be scared of. Make a sizable bet to win the pot right away.

Whenever you perceive an opponent is scared of the board, confirm his fears and bet out. If your opponent makes a mistake, make him pay. Do not let him get away with any mistakes. Even if you do not win a particular hand, in the end you will benefit by exploiting every mistake. In the preceding example, many players would check to take advantage of a free card in hopes of hitting the inside straight or pairing their hole card. By doing this, you are letting your opponent off the hook for a mistake. Your odds of winning the pot right now with a decent bet are much greater than you hitting the inside straight. Even if you do pair one of your hole cards, you may be in trouble. Your opponent may be playing KK, in which case he will have you beat. In addition, if your opponent has QQ, JJ, KQ, or KJ, the card that pairs you may give him a set or a straight.

Remember, in this situation you are taking advantage of your opponent's mistake. You are playing your opponent and the situation, not your cards. Your cards are of secondary importance. If you are playing your cards, then you still need help. However, if you are playing your opponent and the situation, you can win the pot with a sizable bet that punishes your opponent for his mistake.

Poker is a fast-moving game in which you must make decisions quickly. You must constantly monitor the action so that when your opponent makes a mistake you are quick to react.

Let me offer an example from a recent $200 buy-in no limit hold'em tournament I played. After we came back from the second break, the blinds increased to $100–$200, which was a significant amount in a tournament in which the average stack was about $1,600. In the first hand back from the break, I was in the small blind and the big blind had not yet returned to his seat. As the cards were dealt, I kept my eye on a player in *middle position* whom I knew to be an aggressive player apt to steal blinds. After he looked at his cards, I observed him eyeing the empty seat of the big blind. Everyone folds to this player, and it is now his turn to act. Again, he looks to the big blind before raising $200 for a total bet of $400. Everyone folds to me. At this point I know I am going to raise no matter what cards I have. In fact, I do not even remember what cards I had (they were not strong), but I do remember carefully looking at them, placing them down, grabbing some chips, and then asking what the bet was (of course I knew what the bet was, but I wanted to project an eagerness to play these cards). I then raised $600 to make it $1,000, and sure enough, the original raiser folded. I never would have made this play if the original raiser had not made the mistake of broadcasting his intentions. He had looked at the empty chair in the big blind not once but twice, so I was sure he was on a steal.

Take what your opponents give you, but also take what you want.

There is an oft-repeated adage in sports that teams will take what their opponents give them. While that is sound advice that has relevance in poker, it is only half the equation. Certainly, a good poker player will take advantage of his opponents' mistakes. The very good player, however, will be more proactive. Not only will he take what his opponents give him, but he will take what he wants. In poker, you must create opportunities to win pots. You must be willing to bet at a pot in order to take it down. This is especially true in no limit play when often the first person to make a big bet at the pot will win it. Being proactive in going after what you want will serve two purposes: First, it will provide you with the opportunity to win pots immediately, although you must be prepared to take some hits. Next, it will send a message that you are not the kind of player who can be pushed around. You will not be giving your opponents anything, thereby keeping them from "taking what their opponent gives them." In the end, this will serve you well. You will be well on your way to becoming a Prince.

For Machiavelli, the Prince should epitomize power. The Prince should not preside over a democracy. Rather, he should rule as he sees fit. He should take those steps necessary to obtain power. Once in power, he should use his position to maintain and increase his power.

The poker table is not a democracy. Too many players will sit down at the table believing that when they get the cards it is their turn to win and that when an opponent gets the cards it is his turn to win. If this were the case, why even play? Or, rather, why not deal all the cards face up and see who has the luck of the draw? Anyone who sits down with the fatalist attitude that whoever gets the best hands will win is destined to lose. Sure, there is a lot of luck in poker. Over the long run, however, the cards will even out. Skill is what separates the winners from the losers over time.

Before you can practice your skill, you must have the proper attitude. From the moment you sit down, you should strive to own the table. You are the leader. You are the supreme ruler. You are the Prince. You are not at a table of equals. Your opponents are your subjects—there for you to rule.

To be the Prince is to dictate the terms of play. You want your opponents to alter their play based on yours. You want them to fear and respect you. You want them to be so consumed with how you are going to play that they cannot control their own play.

How do you accomplish this? By attacking your opponents' weaknesses, exploiting their vulnerabilities, and punishing their mistakes. If you remain vigilant in doing these things, you will soon find yourself the ruler of the table. Stay completely involved in the game at all times so that you can act when the opportunity presents itself. Mix up your play effectively to keep your opponents from getting a read on you. While your ultimate goal is to maximize your profits, to accomplish this you must first exert control over your opponents. In order to win money, you must defeat your opponents. To defeat your opponents takes more than just cards. You must outplay them. You must understand their play and keep them from understanding yours. If you understand their play and they do not understand yours, they will make mistakes, which you must exploit. Exploit their vulnerabilities and punish their mistakes, and your opponents will respect and fear you. They will recognize you as the leader. As the leader, you can dictate the terms of play.

Once in power, do not let up. Step up the pressure in order to maintain and increase your power. Once you establish yourself as the Prince of the table, your advantage increases exponentially. Opponents will look to you to lead and will be afraid to challenge you.

While Machiavelli wrote of power in the political context, one aspect of power extends well beyond the political arena. The incumbent has a great advantage. Once in power, the incumbent can use his position to influence others. Even though he will face frequent challenges, he will possess an inherent edge against all comers. Until he is displaced, all others will respect and fear the power he can wield from his position. This is just as true in poker as it is in politics. Once established as the ruler of the table, opponents will fear and respect this leader until he is displaced. They will alter their play around the leader's play until they no longer fear that going up against the leader is a losing proposition. The fear of losing money is tough to overcome. It is human nature to want to avoid getting beat.

To be the Prince is to be everything your opponents are not. Let your opponents be overcome with greed or fear. Let your opponents go on tilt. You be the one to maintain your composure and not to lose sight of your goal no matter what the circumstances. When your opponents have a strong hand but yours is stronger, let them bet into you. When your opponents are taken aback by the appearance of scare cards, exploit that to your advantage. Let your opponents play by the book. You be the one to mix up your play and manipulate your opponents' conventionalities. Let your opponents play their cards. You be the one to play the entire situation.

You be the one to lay down strong but losing hands. You be the one to take the pot when no one has a hand. Let your opponents be weak. You be strong.

It is only the strongest of players who can challenge and obtain power. These players must overcome their fears and exert control over their adversaries. They rise to the top no matter what the circumstances present. They overcome all obstacles. They have *virtù*.

III

Virtù

Prevalent in all of Machiavelli's writings is the concept of *virtù*. Machiavelli admired virtù above any other trait a person could possess. Without virtù, one could not have power. For Machiavelli, virtù was the essential charac-teristic necessary in order to obtain and retain power. It is what separated leaders from the rest of the pack. Few have virtù and even fewer are capa-ble of employing it to its full potential on a consistent basis.

What is virtù? There is no direct modern-day English translation. What is clear is that it is not quite the same as the English virtue. While virtue connotes an aspiration to a higher moral good, for Machiavelli one who possessed virtù would do what was politically expedient. What virtue and virtù have in common is that they both descend from the Latin *virtus* that means strength or manliness. (The Latin root *vir* means man.) This defin-ition is how Machiavelli begins in his use of the word virtù.

However, for Machiavelli, virtù is much more. It is alternatively courage, intellect, cunning, skill, determination, resiliency, ambition, toughness, ability, and prowess. It is what a Prince possesses and others do not.

Courage

You cannot play poker with fear. If you are afraid to lose, you cannot win. Do not play in a higher stakes game than you can afford. Poker is a game of calculated risks. If you have zero risk tolerance, you cannot be successful. You must be willing to take on an amount of risk that will provide you with a positive expected rate of return. That is, you must be willing to make bets on a consistent basis that will be profitable over the long run— even if there is a decent chance that you will lose a particular bet. For example, say you are playing seven card stud and you start with a pair of aces. You do not improve, and you are fairly certain that your opponent who is heads-up with you has two small pair. However, your first three up cards are all hearts, and you believe your opponent thinks you are on a flush draw. There is $20 in the pot, and your opponent checks to you on the river. You believe that if you make a $5 bet, there is a 3–1 chance your opponent will fold. Even though you only have a 33 percent chance of winning, you should go ahead and bet because if you do win you will be getting paid 4–1. While it is more likely than not that you will lose this hand, if you make this bet consistently in this situation, you will be profitable over the long run.

If you never take a risk, not only will you miss out on favorable proposition bets, but your play will become very predictable. If you only bet winning hands, you will soon find that you do not get any callers. This is not a profitable way to play poker.

Do not play timidly. If you have a chance to win a pot with a bet, do it. If you sense weakness in your opponents, be proactive. Always play the entire situation, not just your cards. If you are playing hold'em and the flop does not help your opponent, then go ahead and bet. In poker, the first person to bet takes the offensive and has the advantage. By betting out, you put your opponent on the defensive and force him to make a decision as to whether he should call. This is especially true in no limit play when you are not limited to how large a bet you can make. In no limit play, do not be afraid to use the force of a large bet to your advantage. In no limit hold'em, the first person to make a large bet usually wins the hand. The player with more courage will be the one who makes that first large bet.

Playing with courage means playing with conviction. Do not give players the chance to suck out on you. If you are playing seven card stud and you start with a pair of aces, bet it hard. Do not let players draw cards to

beat you. If opponents insist on drawing out, make them pay. Do not give
them free cards.

Do not play it safe. Playing it safe is a losing proposition. Your play will
be predictable and your opponents will use that to their advantage. Take
risks. Mix up your play. Keep your play unpredictable. Dictate the terms
of play. Force your opponents on the defensive.

Intellect

Playing with courage does not mean playing with reckless abandon. It
means doing those things that are calculated to maximize your profits in
the long run. You should not abandon your intellect in your pursuit of
courage. Use your intellect in tandem with courage. You cannot play
courageously without an appropriate appreciation of the risks involved. If
you do not comprehend the risks, you are playing recklessly, not courageously.

Play smart. No matter what game you are playing, make sure you have
a firm grasp of what constitutes a playable hand in every situation. Know
the odds of improving your hand so that you can properly calculate pot
odds. Know what your opponents are likely to be playing and what the odds
are for them to improve. You should be completely aware of all the factors
affecting the game at all times. Only then can you make a conscientious
decision as to how you should act.

Act only when you perceive an advantage. An advantage can come in
many forms. You may have a strong hand. You may sense weakness in
your opponent. Pot odds may be in your favor. You may be able to use position to your advantage. Never underestimate the importance of position
in poker, and never act until it is your turn to act. You never know when
you will be given an opportunity to win a hand. Say you are playing seven
card stud and the low card has to open. In this particular hand, the
low card is to your immediate left, putting you in last position. After he
opens for the minimum amount, everyone folds to you. Now even though
you do not have a strong hand, this may be an opportunity for you to
steal the *antes*. However, if you have already decided that you were going
to fold after looking at your cards before it was your turn to act, you prob-

ably have a *tell* that gave away your intentions, and you have missed that opportunity.

No matter what cards you receive, never make up your mind until it is your turn to act. Only then will you have all the available information needed to make as informed a decision as possible. Give yourself every chance to win. Act only after you have garnered as much information as you can. If you do not perceive an advantage once you have all the available information, then either check or fold as the case may be. Do not commit any money to the pot, if you do not perceive an advantage. Get out of the hand. Save your money to use when you do have an advantage. The money you do not lose is just as valuable as the money you win.

Stay intellectually honest. Do not let superstitions or a bad beat alter your perspective. If you are having a bad run, do not think it is going to change if you move to another seat or if a new dealer comes to the table or if they change the deck. Poker can be a streaky game. If you are on a losing streak, take a minute to evaluate your play. If you determine that you have been playing poorly, then perhaps you should walk away from the table and take a break. However, if you have been playing well but find players are drawing out on you on hands they never should have been in, then maintain your focus. Sometimes in poker you can do everything right but win. If an opponent wants to call your bets in hopes of catching their miracle card, be happy he is your opponent. Even if he hits that miracle card, do not let the bad beat affect your play. In the end, you will win lots of money from an opponent like this if you maintain your composure and stay intellectually honest. Whether or not you are winning or losing, do not get overly confident or despondent. Ignore the short-term ebbs and flows of the game, and keep focused on your long-term goal. If you implement your intellect consistently, regardless of the circumstances, you will be successful.

Cunning

To exercise cunning is more than just bluffing. It is about outplaying your opponent. In poker, to be cunning is to conceal information from your opponent so that he cannot make an informed decision. You conceal information by mixing up your play, hiding strengths, and feigning weakness. When your opponent cannot figure out your play, he cannot completely control his own play. Whenever your opponent has misinformation or less information than he would like, he cannot make an informed decision and his mistakes will increase.

Poker is a game of imperfect information. No matter what form of poker you are playing, there is information each player will not have access to. There are down cards. If any player could see all the down cards, he would have an overwhelming advantage. While this sounds completely obvious, it is amazing how many players will turn their cards over when they do not have to. Even though the hand is over, they are still giving all their opponents access to information that they do not have privilege to. These players are revealing how they play. They have given their opponents information, which the opponents can now use against them.

Whenever a player knows what cards another player is likely holding, he has a tremendous advantage. As a poker player, you have the dual goals of concealing your hand and trying to decipher your opponents' hands. You must use cunning to accomplish both. Mix up your play to hide your hands. Do not always do the same thing in the same situation. For instance, do not always try to steal the blinds in hold'em when everyone folds to you on the button. Challenge your opponents to see what they are holding and how they are playing. Outfox your opponent. Always think ahead. Think more than just one move ahead. Think about hands down the road. Make a bluff on the river knowing you may get called. Even if you have to reveal your bluff, it will pay off for you later when you bet the river with the *nuts*. Remember how an opponent played a certain hand so that you can use that information later. On the very rare occasion, reveal a hand when you do not have to if you are trying to project a certain image. Maybe you want to show that you can lay down a strong hand in order to induce a bluff on your opponent's part later on.

Deception in poker is much more than an isolated bluff. The entire game is a give and take of concealing information and trying to decipher information. It is an ongoing process. Every move you make should keep these goals in mind. Even when you know you are going to fold, there will be times when you want to pretend you are deliberating very hard before you fold. For example, if you just tried to steal a hand with a bluff and your opponent comes over the top with a big raise, you know you have to fold. However, if you fold immediately, everyone will know you were trying to steal. If you really take your time and deliberate, then it looks like you really had a hand. Even though it will not help you in the present hand, it may allow you to steal a pot later on.

Most of the deception in poker is subtle, not overt. Some of the best bluffs are implemented by inaction rather than action. Inducing a bluff on the river is one of the most effective and difficult forms of deception to implement. It takes guts to execute, because if you fail, you have lost your last opportunity to make a bet. However, if you succeed, it will pay off exponentially more than a bet on your part would have. The ultimate example of this is Johnny Chan's play in the final stages of the 1988 *World Series of Poker®*.

They were playing no limit hold'em. Chan was heads-up with Erik Seidel when he flopped the nut straight. Chan held J♣, 9♣ and the flop was Q♠, 10♦, 8♦. Seidel held a Queen with a weak kicker giving him top pair. There was $40,000 in the pot, and Chan was first to act after the flop. He checked. Seidel bet $50,000, which Chan called. The turn brought a *blank* and again Chan checked. However, this time Seidel checked also. The river brought another blank and again Chan checked. This time Seidel went *all-in* and, of course, Chan called. Seidel was severely crippled, and shortly thereafter Chan was world champion. Chan took a big chance by checking on the river. If Seidel had also checked, then Chan would have lost the opportunity to make a bet with the nuts. However, by checking his last opportunity to bet, Chan projected weakness that he hoped Seidel would seek to exploit. Seidel did, and Chan maximized his profits. Certainly, if Chan had gone all-in first, Seidel would have folded.

Skill

While poker is a simple game to learn how to play, it is a difficult game to learn how to play well. It requires a lot of time and practice to hone your skills. The best way to improve is to play often. So long as you stay within your means, try to test yourself against increasingly better competition. If you are consistently successful at $6–$12 hold'em, then try moving up to a $10–$20 game. The only way to improve is to play against the best competition you can afford. Do not play, however, if it is not cost effective. Not only will you lose money, but you will damage your game. Your confidence will erode, and soon you will be playing not to lose and your skills will deteriorate.

Do not be afraid to experiment. Try out unorthodox moves to see how they work for you. Test your opponents as well as yourself. Every player has his own unique style. Find a style of play that is comfortable and works for you. Observe the games of other players, and do not be afraid to ask questions. You will find most poker players are happy to discuss strategy. Seek out those who offer honest advice. Take note of both strong and weak play to see what is successful and what is not.

While you can and should incorporate various things that you observe from other players into your own game, avoid emulating a player whose style is not suited for you. For example, some players are very successful at being super aggressive in no limit hold'em. However, very few people are capable of playing that way, and there are plenty of successful no limit hold'em players who are not overly aggressive. Play a style that works for you.

Try many different poker games. While fundamental poker strategy is applicable to all of poker, the skills involved in the various games are as diverse as the games themselves. While it seems obvious that stud is a very different game from Omaha, even within the same game, there are dramatic differences. For instance, no limit hold'em is a very different game from limit hold'em. Stud hi-lo is a very different game from stud. Play them all to see what works best for you. Most likely, you will have a couple of favorite games that you will concentrate on. However, you should periodically play even those games you do not like as much. It will help keep you fresh and raise your overall skill level. The different perspective you gain will help you when you go back to your favorite game. If you play the same game all the time, you will tend to fall into specific habits. Playing another game will force you to concentrate harder and examine your overall play.

Play both tournaments and *ring games* (also called *side or cash games*). The strategy involved in tournament play is extremely different from a ring game. Play them both. While the skills involved are different, playing both will help your overall game. For instance, if you cannot afford to move up from the low-limit tables, but you want to play against better competition, try a tournament. Not only will you find better competition, but everyone will be playing on an equal playing field. Once you pay your tournament fee, everyone starts with the same amount of chips. You do not have to worry about playing against someone with deep pockets.

No matter what your game or skill level, poker is an ongoing process. So long as you are playing, you should strive to improve. Poker is an extremely complex and subtle game. Each game is unique. The situation changes with each hand. Opponents, cards, seat position, and chip stacks are in a constant state of flux. The potential plays are infinite, offering you a never-ending opportunity to improve your skills.

Determination

In poker, as with any pursuit, determination goes a long way. However, since poker is a subtle game, the determination required is different. Unlike a Prince, you cannot overwhelm your opponents. Unlike modern day politics, you cannot just outspend your opponents. Try to outspend your opponents in poker, and you will go broke.

The determination you need in poker is one of patience and hard work. You must be willing to work constantly on your game. Always strive to improve your skills, and do not expect immediate results. Have the patience to give your skills a chance to work. Have the patience to keep your emotions under control. Poker can be a frustrating game. After a bad beat, it is natural to want to get back at your opponent. However, poker is not a physical game. Unlike football, you do not benefit by taking your frustrations out on your opponent. Remember that. I have seen too many players go on tilt after a frustrating bad beat. They somehow believe they can beat their opponent into submission by betting a lot and often.

If you really want to beat your opponent, then practice the determination required in poker. Stay focused and in control and look for opportunities to exploit your opponent's mistakes. Be patient, and know that your skills will eventually win out. In poker, determination requires the discipline to stay within your game so you can accomplish your goal.

Resiliency

Due to the arbitrary and capricious nature of card distribution, poker can be an extremely frustrating game. In the short term, anybody can beat anybody. There have been times when I have sat at a table to find one player on tilt. This player is the ideal opponent. He is a calling station. He plays every hand to the river and then folds when he does not make a hand. If you play every hand, you are going to lose a lot of money, but you will also make a lot of hands just because you are playing them all. Of course, it seemed like the only time this calling station made a hand was when he was heads-up with me. Everyone else at the table seemed to be making money off this player except me. If I hit a straight, he would make a flush. If I started with aces, he would make two small pair by the river and I would not improve.

What could I have done? Nothing but stay focused and determined. As I mentioned earlier, there will be times when you do everything right but win. Poker requires a great deal of resiliency. If you allow a bad beat to frustrate you, you will not last long in poker. Whenever you find yourself down at a table, you should evaluate how well you have been playing. If you have been playing well and have been up against weak opponents, then stay the course. Be patient and play your game. The pots will eventually come. If on the other hand, you are not playing well, or you are coming up against some very good competition that you just cannot handle at the moment, get up and leave. Take a break. If you come back later, try a different table.

Be resilient but not stubborn. Be aware of how well you are playing and whom you are playing against. Every player is going to have times when he is being outplayed. Learn from your mistakes but learn quickly. If you are outgunned, get up and leave. The more you lose, the greater the disadvantage. Chip stacks are power. If you are not in power and unlikely to gain power, do not play the subject to someone else's Prince.

Ambition

If you do not want to win, you will not win. Even if you are a purely recreational player, why are you playing poker? To win. Poker is a game measured in dollars and cents. You are either up or down. It is not like golf, where you can measure up against yourself. There are no handicaps in poker. There are no moral victories either. *Si guarda al fine*—one judges by the result. At its core, poker is the most base and ruthless of contests. It is the perfect arena for pure unadulterated ambition. Your goal is to beat your opponent and take his money.

You are not a bad person for wanting to succeed at poker. In fact, you owe it to both yourself and your opponents to play with all due earnestness. Poker is a competition. Play to win.

Toughness

Inherent in Machiavelli's definition of virtù is the concept of manliness. However, Machiavelli did not intend for the concept to be exclusive to men. Rather, in keeping with the thinking of his time, toughness was considered a masculine trait. Whether you are a man or a woman, toughness is required to be a successful poker player. Do not let other players push you around. A poker game is a power struggle. Each player strives to be the leader of the table so that he can dictate the terms of play. The player in power has a supreme advantage.

Size up your opponents. Know whom you are up against. Find your opponents' weaknesses so that you can exploit them to your advantage and seize power. Take control of the table.

Poker is a marathon rather than a sprint. It requires endurance. Rarely will you sit down to a poker table for just one hour. You will usually play hours on end. Tournaments, which are becoming more and more popular, can last all day with very few breaks. Championship tournament events will often be at least twelve hours a day for up to six days in a row. Over the course of a poker session or tournament, there will be numerous ebbs and flows. Players will come and go from the table. Your chip stack will go up and down. Power will change hands many times.

To be successful over the long term, you must have the toughness to adapt to the ever-changing circumstances. You must be able to play when you are both in power and out of power. You must be able to play against both weak competition and strong competition. You must be able to play when you have a chip lead and when you are *short-stacked*. You must be able to play when you are getting cards and when you are not getting cards. You must have the toughness to implement all the qualities of virtu consistently all the time.

Ability

Know your ability and play within it. Have confidence in your ability. Most importantly, give your ability the chance to win. Poker can be an excruciatingly slow game. It is a game that requires a lot of patience. To be impatient undermines your ability. Do not play a hand after an hour that you would have avoided playing when you first sat down. For example, if you are playing hold'em and have not seen a playable hand in quite some time, avoid the temptation to play Q, 7 suited. Whether you have been playing five minutes or five hours, you should only be playing hands when you perceive an advantage. To do otherwise is to rely on luck rather than your ability. Rely on your ability. You have worked hard to improve your skills and reach an ability level that provides you with an advantage over your opponents. Do not throw away that advantage. Be patient and give your ability the chance to conquer your foes.

Prowess

Your prowess is the culmination of all the other factors embodying virtù. It is your complete package. It is the image you will want to project to your opponents. It is what will help you deal with the biggest obstacle facing all poker players—the randomness of Fortune.

IV.

Fortune

During Machiavelli's time, the accepted wisdom was that one's fate was predetermined. In a predominately Christian society, many thought that God's will governed everything. Whether the setting was war, politics, or economics, few people believed that individuals controlled their own destiny. While Machiavelli had a less fatalistic view of destiny, he did believe in Fortune. (Fortune is capitalized here because it references Machiavelli's use of Fortune or Fortuna—the Roman goddess of luck.)

Machiavelli's view of Fortune was a pessimistic one as well as one that is apropos to poker. Machiavelli believed that no matter what course of action an individual embarked on, he was sure to run into problems both random and unknown. Such is the capriciousness of the world. Furthermore, little could anyone do to prevent such problems. Where Machiavelli differed from most thinkers of his day, however, is that he believed an individual could control those aspects of his life when Fortune did not intervene as well as prepare for problems in order to mitigate the impact of Fortune when she did intervene.

Machiavelli even went so far as to quantify the effect of Fortune on one's everyday life. He ascertained that Fortune was responsible for approximately half of one's actions with the individual responsible for the other half. While I am not sure how accurate that statement is in everyday life, I am sure that anyone who has played a lot of poker will agree that it is a fair assessment of life at the poker table.

If having half of your fate left to destiny seems like a high percentage, well it is. The flip side, however, is that an equally large percentage is controlled by you. In fact, the more experienced players can significantly limit Fortune's role in the outcome of their play. However, no matter what your level of play, Fortune is sure to make her presence known, for better or worse. How you deal with her will go a long way in deciding how successful a poker player you can become.

How can you limit the effect of Fortune? Do not give her a chance to come into play. If you consistently mix up your play, study your opponents, analyze the situation, and look for opportunities to exploit, your skill will eventually win out. When you are playing the entire situation and not just your cards, then you gain a big advantage. If you keep your emotions under control and do not let either losing streaks or winning streaks affect your play, you will not fall victim to Fortune's spell.

Do not give Fortune a chance to come into play.

You should be playing poker because you think you have enough skill to be successful. If you want to rely on chance, play craps or roulette instead. While this seems like a simple enough concept, it is amazing how many players will unwittingly leave much too much to chance rather than take matters into their own hands.

If someone offered you the opportunity to play ten hands of cards and you could choose between a guaranteed $10 profit from each hand or, alternatively, a 30 percent chance at $20 in each of the ten hands, which would you choose? If you took the guaranteed $10 per hand, you would win $10 times 10 hands for a total of $100. If you chose to gamble, on average you would win the $20 a total of 3 times every 10 hands for a total of $60. It is really not much of a choice.

While this illustration is obvious, it is analogous to many poker plays. If you are dealt pocket aces playing hold'em, you are an overwhelming favorite heads-up with another opponent. However, if there is a *multiway pot* with five players, you are an *underdog* against your opponents collectively. Yet time and again, you will see players *slow play* aces before the flop and let a number of opponents *limp in*. Why? The more players in the pot, the more likely it is that someone will hit the flop or at least get a good draw. At that point you are very vulnerable. What if the flop came 9♣, 6♣, 10♥? The number of hands that could beat you are as numerous as they are varied. An opponent holding any of the following very playable hands could beat you: 6-6, 9-9, 10-10, 9-10, J-Q, or any two clubs. What is worse is that it will be very tough to lay down your aces in the face of this flop. If someone makes a hand, you are vulnerable to losing a lot of money.

On the other hand, what do you stand to gain by slow playing aces? If you manage to hit an ace on the flop, you are unlikely to get any callers unless one of your opponents has the fourth ace. You are really hoping someone flops top pair (and a high pair at that) or tries to steal the pot. The risk/reward ratio is just not worth it. It is much better to play your aces strong from the beginning. Weed out the drawing hands. Get heads-up with somebody or win the pot right there. If you do get a number of callers after raising with aces, then you are likely to be up against smaller pairs or high aces. In either event, these hands pose far less risk to you (as opposed to drawing hands such as suited connectors) as they will have fewer *outs*.

Anytime you offer opponents the chance to *draw out* on you, you are leaving your fate in the hands of Fortune. Never give opponents free cards. If they want to *chase* runners, make them pay. One of the biggest mistakes beginning players make is feeling that it is too risky to bet a lot of money early in a hand even if they have the high hand. They are worried that someone can beat them, and they do not want to lose too much money. If you are playing seven card stud and you start with a high pair, you have to bet it. Unless you have the nuts, you should just about always bet the best hand. You want to weed out the field. You do not want players chasing you. It is much riskier not to bet it hard. If you bet it hard, you will either win the hand right there or gain information. If an opponent calls, he either has a strong hand or is a calling station. You should be able to know based on how your opponents have been playing. Whenever you gain information, you gain an edge. The more information you have, the less you leave to chance.

Study your opponent.

Know your opponent. Study his play. Test him. Probe and observe. Know how he reacts to certain situations. Know which hands he likes to play, bet, raise, and fold. Poker is a game of imperfect information. The more information you can ascertain, the less you leave to chance. When you can determine what hand(s) your opponent is likely playing, you can make an informed decision as to what to do. This does not mean that every decision will be easy or that Fortune will be entirely eliminated. However, it allows you to calculate the risk and make a decision based on that risk. When you are able to do this, you are adequately protecting yourself against Fortune. You do not know how she is going to respond in any given hand, but you know that so long as you can accurately calculate the risk, you will be successful over the long run.

Machiavelli compared Fortune to a flooding river with the potential to drown everything in its path. While one would seem helpless to combat this description of Fortune, Machiavelli believed otherwise. He advocated exercising caution and proper planning to deal with the problem. For instance, by building dams and channels, man could prevent the river from flooding and causing mass destruction. Certainly, if you live in a flood zone, you know of the potential risks and you will plan accordingly.

In poker, you know if you do not have the nuts, you are vulnerable to a higher hand. Plan accordingly. Do not guess when there is information readily available that could help you. If you are playing seven card stud, make sure you take note of every card even if it may not seem relevant at the time. For instance, if you are dealt three spades, most players will take a quick look around to see if there are any other spades face up. While this is immediately helpful and useful information now, you need more than that. You do not know what cards will be relevant later on. Use a little foresight here. You may hit your Jack-high spade flush and find yourself up against a potential heart flush. It would be nice to know how many hearts are folded and, specifically, whether the ace, King, or Queen of hearts is still out there. When playing seven card stud, a good habit to get into is to look at everyone else's cards before you look at your own. Your cards are not going anywhere. You do not want to be looking at your cards while other players are folding before you have had the opportunity to witness their cards.

Analyze the situation.

Machiavelli cautioned that the world is a constantly evolving place. In order to be successful, people have to adapt to the ever-changing circumstances. While someone could be successful employing a certain method, if he never changes that method, then eventually he will fail.

The one constant in poker is change. Players come and go from the table, chips change hands, players change seats, and opponents mix up their play. Just the presence of one of these changes can make a dramatic difference. If an extremely aggressive player joins what has been an otherwise very tight game, the entire game will change. Not only must you take into account this new player's aggressiveness, but you must take into account how every other player will react to that player's aggressiveness. What worked five minutes ago may not work now. You must adapt to the new circumstances. The situation has changed. You must analyze what needs to be done. To do otherwise is to leave too much to chance. If you play your cards regardless of your opponents and the situation, you are, in essence, hoping that Fortune will smile on you. If you are feeling that lucky, go play craps.

While it is always dangerous to generalize, there are a few rules of thumb that typically hold true. For instance, anytime a new table gets started, the players will start out very conservatively. There are a number of reasons for this. Some players want to feel each other out. Others are cautious about employing chips so soon, especially when they see no one else doing it. Finally, there will be some players sticking to their renewed vow to play disciplined and not go on tilt. However, inevitably the table will loosen up. Players get bored, relax, and go on tilt. Everyone feeds off each other. As soon as you get your first big pot, things will change quickly. Keep this in mind so you can adjust accordingly. In addition, study every new player who sits down to a table. Typically, they will play very cautiously at first until they feel they are in the flow of things.

Let your opponents deal with Fortune.

Mix up your play. If you can minimize Fortune's impact by knowing how your opponent plays, it follows that your opponent can also minimize Fortune's impact by understanding your play. Do not give him that opportunity. Mix up your play. Employ deception. Feign weakness. Do not always do the same thing in the same situation. If you always fold your big blind, you invite players to steal. Defending your big blind on occasions even when you have marginal cards will benefit you in the long run. When your opponent has to guess at your play, you force him to rely on Fortune.

By adapting to the ever-changing circumstances, you will naturally be mixing up your play. However, an astute opponent will be equally aware that you have adapted, and he will adjust accordingly. Therefore, mixing up your play requires something more. It requires employing some unorthodox plays to keep your opponents from gaining a read on you. When you have position on a weak opponent, play some medium-strength hands aggressively. Even if you are called down and lose, you benefit by having all your opponents see what appears to be loose play on your part.

Implement some semi-bluffs. Say you are playing seven card stud and start with a pair of Kings. By fifth street you have not improved, but your three exposed cards are all hearts (and your two down cards are not hearts). You are heads-up with an opponent who you believe is playing aces. Go ahead and bet or raise. If you get another heart on sixth street, you will, in all likelihood, win the pot right there. By betting or raising, you have given yourself more outs. Your opponent is now afraid of a flush, even though you were playing a pair of Kings. Although a heart on sixth street will not complete your flush, your opponent will believe it does.

If you find it difficult to mix up your play, there are some things that you can do that are relatively easy yet still effective. For instance, before you sit down, choose a playable (but not strong) hand that you will play with strength. If you are playing hold'em, choose a hand like 10, 8 suited. This will allow you to mix up your play naturally without overthinking. Your decision is already made for you. Since the times that you receive 10, 8 suited will be completely random, your play will appear unpredictable, even though you are playing with discipline and organization.

While you want to give your opponent as little information as possible, you also want to give him misinformation. Project a false image. While you typically never want to show your hand when you do not have to, show your cards on very rare occasions if you believe it will help you. If you are a very tight player, play a medium hand aggressively and show your cards. Anything you can do to confuse your opponent will help you. The more doubts he has about your play, the more you force him to rely on Fortune. You play good poker. Let your opponent deal with Fortune.

When you are blindsided by Fortune, how do you react?

No matter how well you play, you can never entirely eliminate Fortune. How you react when Fortune is not smiling on you will go a long way in determining what kind of poker player you are.

Stay focused, and keep your emotions under control. Do not panic. Do not go on tilt. The worst hand Fortune can deal you is, of course, a bad beat. You find yourself with an overwhelming favorite, and you bet it strong. Your opponent calls when he is not only a big underdog, but he is not even getting pot odds to do so. Yet, somehow, that miracle card lands on the river making your opponent's hand and crushing yours. What can you do? The answer is absolutely nothing. Tell your opponent nice hand, muck your cards, and get ready for the next hand.

You have to remember to take the bad with the good. Your ideal opponent is a calling station. Well, a calling station is going to draw out on you sometimes. That is poker. Do not get upset. Remember your long-term goals. Poker is a marathon, not a sprint. What is important is how well you do overall. And overall is not one poker session or one day or even one week. Depending on how often you play, you should measure how well you do over months or even a year. You owe it to yourself to give your play a chance to win free of the influence of Fortune. Over the long run, Fortune's effect will even out. In the short term, however, she can run roughshod over you. When that happens, concentrate on minimizing your losses rather than trying to make all your money back in a hurry. If you try to win all your money back in a hurry, you play right into Fortune's hand. You are relying on luck and creating an even playing field with your inferior opponents.

Do not play down to your opponent's level of play. Stay disciplined no matter how lucky your opponent gets or no matter how many bad beats you suffer. If you keep receiving trash hands in hold'em, resist the urge to go in with 6, 8 off-suit from the small blind when there is a raise and a couple of other callers ahead of you. This hand can only get you in trouble. If you get a piece of the flop, you will be tempted to play a very vulnerable hand since you have not seen much action. Do not allow yourself to be sucked in and to compound an initial mistake. Rather, be patient and keep doing those things that make you successful. Stay aware of the situation, and notice how it is affecting you. If you find yourself down a lot, make sure you are not playing scared. If you are, get up and leave. Take a break. If you want to play later, play a lower limit table. Do not judge your play based on one day's outcome.

Fortune can work both ways. If you find yourself consistently getting good hands, keep it in perspective. By all means use the rush to your advantage to intimidate and exploit your opponents. However, do not allow yourself to feel a false sense of security. Fortune is fickle and she can turn in an instant. As soon as you feel invincible, you will be raising your strong second-best hand against the stone-cold nuts, and you will lose a lot of money.

Machiavelli recognized that there were different ways that one could obtain power. One way was through prowess. Another way was by Fortune. At the poker table, you will see players become the leaders of their table via both of these means. The player who obtains power by means of prowess, however, is the player to be admired. The player who has used his skill to take control of the table is the player most likely to maintain his ruling position. Fortune is unpredictable, and she can cause a player to fall from power just as easily as she can help him obtain it.

Be aware of how the leader or leaders of your table have obtained their position. How you deal with one who has used his prowess as opposed to the leader who has had good Fortune is markedly different. In addition, recognize how much of a factor Fortune is playing in your position at the table. Even if you possess prowess, there will be times when Fortune will propel you to the top. You must recognize this in order to understand how your opponents will perceive you.

Whether you are running hot or cold, stay within your game. Do not be intimidated by Fortune. Rather, do everything in your power to ensure that skill, not luck, will be the determining factor when you play poker. You do not need to rely on luck. You have free will.

v.
Free Will

Prior to Machiavelli, Medieval and Renaissance philosophers accepted the notion of divine destiny as the explanation for every imaginable disaster. They did not believe man possessed the power to prevent a calamity preordained from a higher being. Machiavelli was one of the first thinkers to take a more pragmatic viewpoint of such events. He was one of the first to express the notion of man's self-determination. Machiavelli had great confidence in man's ability to set his own destiny in the face of a whole range of obstacles whether or not such obstacles, came from above. Machiavelli believed in man's free will.

While free will seems like a simple and accepted notion in this day and age, it is amazing how few people practice it in every aspect of their lives. There is a tendency to accept things rather than change things. There is a tendency to feel trapped rather than to fight. There is often resignation rather than indignation.

Nowhere is this truer than at the poker table. How many times have you heard a player ask for a new deck or a change in dealers? How often do you see a player change seats in the belief that his seat is unlucky? How many times have you seen a player grumble about a bad beat only to turn over cards he never should have played in the first place?

What do these players all have in common? They believe that their fate at the poker table is out of their hands. Whether it is providence, religion, luck, or some other force, they believe that they do not have control over the outcome. They do not believe in their own free will. If you do not wholeheartedly believe in your own free will at the poker table, you will never be successful.

You have free will. Exercise it. Play smart, disciplined poker. Do not play hunches and whims. Use position and tells. Do not use good luck charms. Change seats to get better position on certain players. Do not change seats for luck. Play the entire situation. Do not blindly play cards.

Play smart, disciplined poker.

As a skillful poker player relying on his prowess and not Fortune, keep your focus on playing consistently smart, disciplined poker. Poker is a very easy game, so your discipline can slip. Remember that a calling station is going to make a number of hands by just staying in every hand. Remember, too, that he is going to lose a lot of money in the end. Again, to repeat, do not play down to your opponent's level.

Do not second-guess yourself when you make a smart, disciplined play. If you play enough poker, there will be plenty of times when you will be kicking yourself for not staying in a hand when you originally made the right decision. For instance, you are playing hold'em, and you are tempted to play J, 9 off-suit in the small blind. In fact, you have made up your mind that you will see this flop for the half bet it will cost you. Then there is a raise from a player who you know to be tight in early position. You think long and hard about calling anyway before you decide to fold. The big blind calls and the flop comes J, J, 9. You are furious at yourself for not calling. Do not be. You made the right decision at the time. If you threw away 2, 7 off-suit under the gun and the flop came 2, 7, 7, would you be mad at yourself? Of course not, because mucking 2, 7 off-suit is a no-brainer. Why, then, should you be mad at throwing away J, 9 off-suit in the small blind? Even if it was a tougher decision, it was still the right decision. If you start to second-guess yourself for making the right decision, your discipline starts to unravel. You may assign J, 9 off-suit more value than it deserves the next time you see it. Or you may call a bet from the small blind with a marginal hand. Or you may start playing hunches. All these things are losing propositions. Rather than unravel, take a deep breath and remind yourself that only a calling station would have played that J, 9 off-suit under those circumstances.

You are better than that. Do not worry about short-term success. If you play smart, disciplined poker on a consistent basis, the long-term result will take care of itself. Si guarda al fine—one judges by the result. On a short-term basis in poker, the result is often out of your control. Poker is a highly competitive environment in which Fortune plays a higher than normal role. What is within your control, however, is free will. Concentrate on the process and not the result. The ability to stay focused and to play smart, disciplined poker no matter what the circumstances will lead to long-term gains. Resist the temptation to stray from your game. Do not play hunches or whims. Do not chase hands just because you have not had a hand to play in a while. Do not get rattled by Fortune. Be patient. In poker one looks to the end result, but that result must take place over an extended period.

Use position and tells.

In exercising free will, you must use every resource available to you. Study your opponents' every hand to pick up information. Poker is a game of imperfect information. The more information at your disposal, the better decisions you can make. To exercise your free will fully, you cannot be ignorant to what is going on around you. You must pick up as much information as possible.

When you are not in a hand, do not disengage. Stay involved, and try to figure out how each remaining player is playing. Put yourself in the position of each player to help you better understand how each one plays. To put yourself in another player's position involves a little playacting on your part. Do not just put yourself in their position and ask yourself what you would do in that situation. Try to ascertain how your opponent will play. Take on his role. If your opponent plays aggressively and has a big stack, then get in that mind-set and determine how you would play his hand. Soon you will find yourself consistently and accurately putting your opponents on hands. Once you are able to do so, your ability to exercise free will will not be hampered by insufficient information.

Use your position at the table to your advantage. If you are playing hold'em and you have a marginal hand, play it from late position if you can get in cheaply. Just be sure to mix up your play. Occasionally, make a strong play from early position in hold'em. This can be a very effective move especially in no limit hold'em. Your opponents are likely to put you on a very strong hand if you make a big bet from early position in hold'em. This gives you a number of ways to win a pot. First, if you have a conservative image, you are likely to win the pot uncontested pre-flop. If you do get a caller, you have two chances to win on the flop. If you either hit the flop or get a scary flop, you are in position to make a substantial bet after the flop. Since the first person to make a substantial bet in no limit play often wins the pot, your early position is an advantage.

Stay engaged in every hand, and do not commit yourself until it is your turn to act. No matter what game you are playing, it is a good practice to study your opponents as the cards are being dealt rather than looking at your cards. This accomplishes two things: First, it affords you the opportunity to pick up tells. Second, it prevents you from projecting any tells or making a decision until it is your turn to act. Wait until everyone in front of you has acted before looking at your cards. At that point, you will have all the available information, and you can make an informed decision. A hand you may not have played at first glance may now be playable depending on how those in front of you have proceeded.

How many times have you played poker and there was one person who consistently raised with nothing? And how many times have you sat there hoping to get a playable hand so that you could challenge him, only to look down at your cards hand after hand and see nothing but garbage? Then, when you finally do get a hand in a heads-up situation with this maniac and you re-raise him, what does he do? He folds, of course. So what does that tell you? You did not have to wait for a premium hand to challenge him. If you know he is going to be super aggressive until someone challenges him, then challenge him. Wait until you have an opportunity to get heads-up with him and then raise him. It does not matter what cards you are holding. You have free will.

You can play any cards in the right situation. In fact, there are situations where you must play no matter what cards you are holding. If the maniac will keep betting until someone stops him, then stop him. Unless he has a very strong hand, he will likely fold. If he does not, then two things can happen: you can get help with the cards to come, or you are ultimately forced to fold. Even if you eventually fold, you have made it clear that you are not afraid to challenge him (even with something less than a premium hand since you folded), and he will think twice about raising you in future hands. The point is you cannot always wait for cards. If you want to be a leader, you must be proactive in establishing your presence at the poker table. This does not mean playing recklessly. It means picking opportune times (with position or scare cards) to challenge vulnerable opponents. It means fighting back so that others do not think they can always force you to fold. It means getting to know your opponents so that you can play them as much as you are playing your cards. Do not be shy about observing players. If other players catch you or give you a look back, do not let this discourage you. You have every right to exercise your free will and gather as much information as possible.

Change seats to get better position on certain players.

To exercise free will, control every aspect of the game that you can. Because you cannot control much in poker, you must take the initiative in those parts of the game that you can control to be successful. This should start before you even sit down. First, choose the game that is right for you. If you are looking for action, do not think that you have to play the biggest game in town. You are likely to be against some very stiff competition. Conversely, do not assume that you can run roughshod over the low-limit games. The low-limit tables are often filled with nonserious players who want to play as many hands as possible. While these calling stations may seem like ideal opponents, if the entire table is composed of these players, luck will play a more dominant role than skill.

Find a table that suits your game. Every person has their own style, so everyone's ideal table will be different. It is up to you to find the table with competition and betting limits comfortable to you, and likely to be profitable for you in the long run. At most casinos you typically choose the game and betting limits you want to play, and then you will be assigned a seat when one becomes available on a first come, first served basis. However, once seated you will be allowed to request a move to any other table as soon as a seat opens there. You will also be allowed to switch seats at your own table should a player vacate.

Why would you want to switch seats at your own table? Certainly, you should not be doing it to change your luck. Any player who asks for a seat change (for luck) or a change of the deck is relying on luck not their own free will in order to succeed. Such a player is destined to fail. You should change seats to get a better position.

It is up to each individual to find a position that is ideally suited to his game and likely to maximize his profits. Most poker theorists will advise that in limit hold'em or Omaha, it is optimum to have the hyperaggressive players to your right and the passive predictable players to your left. The logic being that you do not want to commit to a pot until you know what the maniac is going to do. If you are willing to limp in but you know it is highly likely the maniac will raise you, then you are at a great advantage having the maniac act before you.

Having the passive players to your left offers you the chance to force them out or steal their blinds. Since their play is more predictable, there is not as big an advantage in having them act before you. While this is solid advice, it may not be for everyone. For instance, playing with the maniac to your immediate right may severely limit the amount of hands that you play. Since he is likely to raise before you even act, you will only play strong hands. Furthermore, when you do play these strong hands, you are vulnerable. You will want to raise in order to get heads-up with the maniac. The players yet to act behind you, however, are likely to know that you are trying to get heads-up. Now if a player behind you re-raises, he is likely to have you beat, and you are caught in between the maniac and the re-raiser.

Thus, you may be better off having the hyperaggressive player a few spots to your right. Personally, I prefer to have the hyperaggressive player across the table from me. That way, he will act before me approximately half the time. When he does, I will not only have the benefit of seeing his actions but also the actions of a number of players after him. The other half of the time, I will get the opportunity to act before the maniac, which I think has its own advantages. Maniacs like to be the aggressors. If someone raises before them, they will often fold a weak hand. So by raising prior to his acting, I send a signal, not only to the maniac, but to the other players as well. Those players between the maniac and me are not likely to call one raise knowing the maniac has yet to act. In addition, if I have a very strong hand, I can let the maniac do my betting for me. Thus, by acting before him at times, I increase the opportunities to exploit his play.

While this is just one example of seat position and only represents my own personal preference, it illustrates the importance of choosing the correct seat. You may not always be able to choose the perfect seat. However, having an awareness of what suits your game and optimizes your profit will allow you to move tables and seats when you have the opportunity and it is advantageous to do so. Be proactive. Exercise free will. Do everything you can in your power to increase your potential profitability. Poker is a game of constant change. Keep abreast of who leaves and comes to your table. What is a good seat at the moment could change dramatically with the addition of one player. Stay aware of the entire situation.

Play the entire situation.

One of the biggest mistakes beginning players make is to play their cards blindly without any thought as to what else is going on. The hardest thing to do in poker is to lay down a strong but losing hand. The ability to do so, however, is what makes a successful poker player. The money you do not lose is as important as the money you win.

Do not get married to a hand. If you are playing hold'em and you are dealt pocket Jacks, you have a strong hand depending on the situation. If everyone folds to you in late position, go ahead and raise, as you can be fairly confident you have the *best of it* now. However, if there are two raises before you from players you know to play tight, you should probably fold your Jacks. The point is that every hand plays differently depending on the situation.

Know the situation. You cannot exercise free will unless you are completely aware of the situation. Know your opponents and know how they play. Know what hands they are likely to be holding. Know how many chips they have on the table. Know if they are up or down and know how that is affecting their play. Recognize when your opponents are vulnerable, but, more importantly, recognize when you are vulnerable.

Many losses can be avoided by the exercise of free will. No one is forcing you to play a particular hand. If you are dealt pocket Kings in hold'em and the flop brings A♥, 9♥, 10♥ and neither one of your Kings is a heart, you should fold them in the face of any bet. Just too many hands can beat you. While this is an obvious example, be aware that whenever the flop goes south for you, exercise caution. A strong starting hand can turn into a vulnerable hand quickly, no matter what game you are playing. If you are playing seven card stud and start with a pair of aces but you are unable to chase away three other opponents, there is a high likelihood that one of them will have you beat if you do not improve.

Play the situation. I can even think of a situation where pocket aces should be folded pre-flop in hold'em. Say you are playing a no limit hold'em tournament, and you are down to the final three players. You are short-stacked with about $20,000 in chips and each of the other players has $490,000 in chips. You find yourself in the big blind with pocket rockets (aces); to your surprise, the player on the button goes all-in and he is quickly called by the small blind. Before you rush your few remaining chips into the pot, analyze the situation. If you fold, you are virtually guaranteed to move into second place money. Unless the other two players are playing the same hand, one of them is sure to be eliminated. If you call, however, you stand a good chance of tripling up. Where would that leave you? In second place with $60,000 in chips against the chip leader who would then have $940,000. If you lose by calling, however, you finish in third place. So is it really worth calling and risking a guaranteed second-place finish for the opportunity to be heads-up with $60,000 in chips rather than $20,000? If you analyze the situation, it is really a simple decision. What at first glance seemed like an obvious play is in actuality a really easy fold.

Every hand is unique. You must play the situation and not just the cards. The cards are just one factor to consider in determining how you should play. There will be times when you play very weak hands that you will sense vulnerability on the part of your opponents. In these situations, you will not be playing your cards but rather your opponents' vulnerability.

There will be times when you will be able to steal blinds because of your position and the weakness of the players in the blinds. Your cards will be of secondary concern. There will be times when you can steal antes in seven card stud when you have nothing but an ace showing.

On the first glance at your cards, avoid getting too excited or too pessimistic. The cards are only one factor. Take the time to analyze the entire situation so that you may exercise your free will to its full potential. Only when you exercise your free will to the fullest extent possible will you be able to ascend to power at the poker table.

VI

Power

If you possess virtù and exercise free will, you will be able to ascend to power at the poker table. While you can also ascend to power through the whim of Fortune, it is far better to get there through means of your own doing. As Machiavelli advised, if you have obtained power through your own merits, it will be much easier to retain your position than if you had achieved it through Fortune. That is not to say that retaining power will be easy. It is just as difficult to retain your position, as it is to obtain it. Machiavelli recognized how difficult it can be for a Prince to retain power. He cautioned that a leader does not want to endure the hatred of the people. When the anger of the people reaches such proportions, the leader will find himself in a precarious position. However, as long as a leader was not hated, Machiavelli did not believe it was necessary for a leader to be loved. In fact, Machiavelli advocated that a leader was better off being feared than loved. This delicate balance of being feared but not hated that Machiavelli counseled for the Prince is apropos for one who aspires to lead the poker table.

It is better to be feared than loved.

Your goal at the poker table is not to be loved and adored by everyone. You are there to make money, and the only way to make money is to win it from your opponents. Certainly, you could not expect to take your opponents' money and have them love you for it. However, you do not want to incur the ire of your opponents either. To do so is to invite them to attack you at every opportunity. While this may cause them to make mistakes, the collective force of their attacks will be hard to overcome. It will be hard to exploit these mistakes when every hand that you want to play finds you up against at least a couple of aggressive and angry opponents. Any leader who has to expend time and effort warding off attacks is vulnerable. It is expended energy that would be put to much better use strategizing and optimizing profit. That is how a leader stays in power.

So how do you accomplish this? It is really quite simple. Maintain a friendly and cordial environment. This is your table. You are the leader. Compliment your opponents. Encourage their mistakes. When an opponent makes an obvious mistake calling you when you clearly had the better hand, tell him that he had to call in that situation and that you would have done the same thing. When your opponent draws out on you in a hand he never should have been in, do not chastise him. Let him know what a tough opponent he is and that you cannot scare him out of a pot. By doing these things, you keep your opponents engaged at the table believing their luck will change at any moment so long as they keep on doing the things that they are doing. To do otherwise creates dissension, and two things can happen—both of them bad: your weak opponents will move to another table, or they will conspire to attack you.

You want your opponents to fear you, not hate you. If you successfully bluff them out of a pot, do not reveal your hand. You do not want to give away free information or show up your opponent. Let him know it was a good lay down on his part. As you continue to outplay your opponents, their respect for your play will grow. They will fear your play and your chip stack. If you are successfully mixing up your play and employing virtu and free will, your opponents will be unable to figure out your play. They will second-guess themselves whenever you are in a pot. They will be unable to control their own play since they cannot figure out yours. They will make mistakes that you can exploit. They will shy away from hands you play, giving you plenty of free pots. In addition, when players do challenge you, you can be confident that they have strong hands, and you can avoid losing large pots.

Maintaining the thin line between fear and hate is a delicate balance. Players will naturally resent an opponent who is taking their money. Conversely, you want to avoid being overly friendly, as you will lose an important intimidation factor. Keep your opponents at a distance but remain civil and cordial. Let your game speak for itself. Retain an element of suspense around you. The unknown is intimidating. Do not reveal yourself or your play.

Knowledge is power.

Poker is a game of imperfect information. Just imagine if you had X-ray vision, and you could see each of your opponent's cards. The game would be simple then, would it not? And what if your opponents could see your cards? You would not stand a chance then, would you? Of course not. But you cannot see your opponents' cards, and they cannot see yours. In fact, you would be extremely angry if you caught someone trying to sneak a peek at your cards. Yet, repeatedly you will see players revealing their hands when they do not have to. They mistakenly believe that no harm can come from revealing their cards once the hand is over. However, nothing could be further from the truth. Every time you reveal your cards, you reveal something about your play. You provide your opponents with information that will make it easier for them to play against you down the road. You provide them with knowledge, and knowledge is power. You give them insight that eventually will provide them with that elusive X-ray vision.

Only reveal your cards when you absolutely have to. Even in a showdown, wait until it is your turn. Not only do you want to avoid unnecessarily revealing your cards, but you want to make sure your opponent reveals his. While this seems simple, the following is an example of the type of situation I witness all the time and the kind of mistake that can be easily avoided with a little discipline. In hold'em, one player bets pre-flop and gets one caller. The bettor continues to bet all the way to the river and he is called each time. The board ends up something like Q♠, 4♥, 7♣, 2♦, 9♠. After the last call, the original bettor does not reveal his cards but instead tells his opponent that a Queen is good. The caller in his excitement turns over his K, Q and gladly scoops up the pot. The original bettor mucks his hand, and the caller misses an opportunity to see his opponent's cards. Not only had the caller every right to see those cards, but he earned that right. He paid for that right. Yet a lack of discipline allowed his opponent to muck his cards. The caller lost information that he paid for.

Obtaining Power

How does one obtain power? To obtain power, one must implement all the skills required of Machiavelli's ideal leader and apply them to the poker forum. Refine all the elements of virtu so that you become a dominant force at the poker table. Be resilient and tough. Implement deception. Play smart and disciplined.

Enter the poker room without any moral reservations. The point of poker is to take your opponents' money by any means necessary (within the rules, of course). Everyone knows, or should know, the score when they sit at the table. It is up to each individual to manage his own funds and gauge how much he can afford to lose. It is not your responsibility to worry about an opponent's losses. Sympathy has no place at the poker table. Poker is a forum in which we can participate in the purest form of competition unequivocally. Everyone is expected to use his cunning and intellect to outwit the others. Anyone willing to pay the entry fee can compete in the top tournaments against the best players in the world. Poker is a truly egalitarian competition.

Be a Prince. Find your opponents' weaknesses and attack them. Exploit your opponents' vulnerabilities. Punish their mistakes. Make the table yours. Your opponents stand between you and success. You must control them. Adopt the mentality of a supreme leader in order to dictate the terms of play.

Keep Fortune in check. Do everything within your power to minimize her effect. Whenever Fortune appears for better or worse, keep her in perspective. Do not get frustrated by bad beats. Do not be tempted to make a bad play when you have not seen a situation to play in quite some time. Do not become overconfident when Fortune is smiling on you.

Exercise free will. Know the fundamentals of poker, but do not always play by the book. Play the situation. Mix up your play. Do not be afraid to try some unorthodox moves. Do not feel limited by position or cards. Study and analyze your opponents. Be aware of how the situation is changing so that you do not miss an opportunity to act. Do not act until it is your turn so that you have the benefit of all the available information. Know all the potential consequences to your actions so that you can make an informed decision.

Make your opponents fear you, but not hate you. Probe your opponents to gather information, but do not reveal information unless forced to do so.

Act boldly.

Poker is a game of imperfect information. Gather as much as you can to make an informed decision, but do not allow yourself to be consumed with the worst-case scenario. Unless you have the stone-cold nuts, the possibility of failure will always exist. Winning poker players recognize this and move on. You can minimize risk, but you cannot eliminate it at the poker table. You will lose sometimes. In the long run, however, you will be much better served by acting boldly than dwelling on all the different ways you can lose. If you are going to play, play with strength. When you act boldly, you put your opponent on the defensive. He is the one who will now be thinking of all the possible hands that can beat him. When you bet or raise judiciously, you project strength and you force your opponent to try to put you on a hand. Unless your opponent has the nuts or a great read on you, you will make him paranoid.

Do not worry about calculating every possible outcome. Boldness can overcome odds. If the best hand always won, all the cards would be dealt face up. Play blackjack if you want to make sure the best hand always wins. If you are going to call, then in the great majority of cases, you should go ahead and bet. Nobody ever won a pot before the river with a call. However, if that same money was put to work by betting rather than calling, you give yourself the chance to win the pot right there.

Retaining Power

If you have obtained power by doing all the things in the preceding section, you will be a strong leader. Your opponents will respect and fear you. You will have earned a substantial advantage by your play. In order to retain power, keep doing everything you did to obtain power.

In addition, take advantage of your position. If you are in power, your opponents will adjust their play to yours. Exploit this. Your force will have increased tremendously. You will have won money, thereby increasing your available resources. Your opponents will have lost money, which may put them on tilt or have them playing scared. In either event, you benefit. Do not let up on your opponents. Push them around. Chase them out of pots. If they are fearful of you, play with intimidation. When they do fight back, you can be fairly certain that they possess strong hands.

When you play from power, you will find it easier to figure out your opponents' play since they will be conforming to you. In addition, your opponents will have a more difficult time understanding your play since they will be playing with fear.

In short, when you are in power, it is your time to make money. Poker is a game of ups and downs. *Si guarda al fine.* One looks to the end result over a long period. You will not always be in power. Plenty of times you will lose money in the short term. Thus, when you are in power, you must do everything within your control to maximize your profits. Do not tighten up. Do not let up on your opponents. Do not rest on your laurels. Exploit your power to the fullest extent possible. Exert your influence over the powerless.

The implementation of power still requires the continuation of smart, disciplined poker. Once you are in power, however, the overall situation changes. The fact that you are in power is an important factor to consider when analyzing the situation. There will be more opportunities to exploit. Opponents will bend more easily to your will.

When you are in a position of power, you should play more hands than usual in order to take full advantage of your position. If you are playing stud, you should always play scare cards until someone pushes back. If you receive an ace up with a 7 and 2 down, raise if no one else does.

When you are the leader, opponents are likely to put you on a better hand than you have. Even if you get some callers, any number of cards you receive on *fourth street* could scare opponents away, even though the card is of no help to you. For instance, any K, Q, J, 10 or card of the same suit as your ace may scare an opponent when you are running hot. If you are playing hold'em or Omaha, take advantage of position to keep attacking your opponents.

You do not want to lose your position of power to inactivity. If you are not getting cards, you must play some marginal hands. Do not let power slip away without a fight. A strong leader will fight with an outmanned army rather than wave the white flag. When you have power, you have an advantage that can be exploited. You are more likely to outplay your opponents. So give yourself the chance to do so rather than let your power slip away.

Keep in mind that as important a factor as your position of power is, it is still only one factor comprising the entire situation. You still must carefully analyze the entire situation as you normally would. As leader, it is up to you to control the play to your advantage while still being aware of all the other factors comprising the situation that could undermine your authority. You must become a master of statesmanship.

VII

Statesmanship

During Machiavelli's time, cities in Italy were in a constant power struggle with their neighbors. War was viewed as unavoidable in the development and defense of city-states. In *The Prince*, Machiavelli took this concept one step further. He believed that the outcome of war would form the foundation on which the city-state was built. If a sound military presence was maintained, good solid laws would naturally follow. For Machiavelli, sound military policy was much more than the implementation of brute force. Military leaders needed to grasp diplomacy, politics, tactical strategy, geography, and history.

A strong military leads to solid laws.

A fundamental concept of any contest is that the party with the most force has a huge advantage. Certainly, this concept is prevalent in poker. The size of your bankroll or chip stack is your force. If you sit down to a table with a smaller stack than the table average, you are at the wrong table. Play a table where you can comfortably bet a large stack. Give yourself an advantage. If you are going to play, play from strength. As mentioned earlier, because so many factors in poker cannot be controlled by you, you must make sure you control those factors which you can.

Find a table that you can easily afford to play. You do not want to sit down at a table with a large chip stack if that stack is more than you can afford to lose. You will be playing scared and without the force of those chips. The chips are not for show. They are your military force, and you must be willing to engage them at any time. It takes chips to make chips. The successful deployment of your force will allow you to accumulate chips from your opponents. Once you do this, you will be forming the foundation of your leadership at the table. You will be establishing the rules of play for your table and controlling your opponents. Your goal is to accumulate as many chips from your opponents as you can at minimal risk to your own chip stack. How do you accomplish this?

If you have the nuts, you do whatever you can to keep your opponents in the pot. You check if a bet will chase them out. You bet if they will call. You check if they will bet. You then raise if they will call or re-raise. When you have the nuts, you want your opponents playing to the showdown. When you do not have the nuts, you do not want a showdown. If you have the best of it, use your chips to chase opponents out and keep them from drawing out on you. If you do not have a strong hand but sense your opponent is vulnerable, then bet to find out if you are right and he folds. If you do not perceive an advantage, then check for a free card or fold to any bet in order to preserve chips.

If you are playing no limit, then your force is only limited by the amount of chips you have in front of you. Use that force as necessary. If your opponent is currently getting pot odds to draw out on you, bet enough so that he is no longer getting those favorable pot odds. For example, say you are playing no limit hold'em and there is $50 in the pot before the flop. The flop comes J♥, 8♥, 3♣. You are holding a pair of tens and bet $10. Two players fold and one calls. You correctly put this caller on a flush draw. He is holding 6♥, 7♥. The turn brings the 2♦, which does not help either of you. With only the river to go, you are approximately a 5–1 favorite. There is $70 in the pot. If you bet $10 (making the pot now $80), your opponent will be getting correct pot odds to call. (He would be getting paid 8–1 on a 5–1 probability.) Thus, the correct thing to do here is to bet a sufficiently high amount to ensure that he does not call. Bet at least $50. With $120 now in the pot, a $50 call on his part will only give him approximately 2.5–1 odds when he is a greater than 5–1 underdog. Now, it is an easy fold for him unless he is a pure gambler in which case you want him in the game.

Chip accumulation takes on added importance in tournament play where everyone starts with the same number of chips. Players cannot reach into their pockets and buy more chips when they are down. Rather, they face elimination. The size of one's chip stack or force thus defines strength at the table.

Do not squander your force. Solid poker strategy requires a delicate balance between chip accumulation and survival. You want to win chips with the least amount of risk. Thus, an overall successful poker strategy is akin to Machiavelli's vision for a successful military strategy. Both require more than the implementation of brute force.

Diplomacy

Win over your opponents. You do not need them to love you, but you do not want them to hate you. You want them to respect your play. You want them to be fearful of your every move. When your opponents fear you, they cannot control their own play. They will adjust their play to your moves or even your anticipated moves. Opponents will be reluctant to join in pots if they do not know whether you will be playing that particular hand. While you want your opponents to fear you, you do not want to engender envy or hatred on their part.

Any successful poker play must include a strategy to manipulate his opponents' emotions. Good, solid, disciplined poker on your part will bring you the respect you want at the poker table. In addition, play with a demeanor and style that will encourage the correct emotions in your opponents. Do not show up your opponents. If you successfully bluff them off a hand, muck your cards. By doing this, you accomplish two things: First, you do not give away free information. Second, you avoid angering your opponent. It is much better to have an opponent fear you rather than have him gunning for you. While neither situation is good for your opponent, you are much better served having a fearful and docile opponent. An angry opponent can become unpredictable and dangerous.

Remember that unless you have the nuts, you are usually better off winning a pot without a showdown. Although one angry opponent on tilt may very well prove profitable for you, many angry opponents could prove disastrous. For example, say you are playing seven card stud and start with a hand such as K♥, 10♣ down and K♣ up. You want to play this hand with strength right from the beginning in order to eliminate as many opponents as possible. While you are likely to be a favorite in a heads-up situation with these cards, if four other players remain, you will be an underdog against your opponents collectively. The more players who remain in the pot, the greater the chance someone will draw out on you. This is particularly true in hi-lo games in which there are more opportunities to improve.

You are playing poker because you believe that your superior skill will win out. Give that skill the chance to win. If you anger your opponents to the point that they will collectively challenge you on every hand, you have managed to diminish the skill factor grimly. With many players in every pot, luck will play a premium. You do not play poker because you are feeling lucky. Again, if you are feeling lucky, go play roulette.

If you are the leader of the table and you are successfully pushing your opponents around (without angering them), eventually one of your opponents will have a strong hand. When he does, respect it. For example, say you are playing $5–$10 seven card stud and you receive 2♥, 6♣ down and the ace of spades up. A few players call the $5 bet before you act. You feel confident that you can win the pot by representing aces with a raise here. However, a player behind you re-raises. Everyone folds to you. Now, you know you are going to fold, but how you fold will make a big difference in maintaining both the right atmosphere and your image. When it is your turn to act, take your time. Pretend you are contemplating. Finally, tell your opponent that you have to fold your three-suited high cards in the face of a tough bet like that. By doing this, you are giving your opponent respect without letting on that you were trying to steal the pot. Your opponent will be proud of himself yet still respect your play. Even if your opponent was bluffing, he will be reluctant to try that again since you took so long to fold and you only had a drawing hand.

Never comment negatively on an opponent's play. Practice diplomacy in order to encourage bad play on your opponent's part. Since it is human nature to believe a compliment, your opponent will continue to play poorly. The added benefit is that you will not anger your opponent.

Maintain a congenial table when you are the leader. Be a benevolent dictator. If your opponents are content, you stand a greater likelihood of enforcing your rules. Keep your opponents fearful but not angry. Be civil to and respectful of your opponents. However, remember that it is your table and that you alone should be dictating the terms.

Say you are playing hold'em, and you have 4♣, J♥ in the big blind and you get one caller. You get to see the flop for free, and the flop comes 5♣, 6♥, 2♦, giving you one *overcard* and an *inside straight draw*. More importantly, you are confident that this flop did not help your opponent who is likely to be playing two overcards. You decide to bet because you can easily represent at least a pair here since you could have anything in the big blind. Your opponent calls. The turn brings 10♣. Again, you bet, and now your opponent folds with what in all likelihood is the better hand. After you muck your hand, your opponent whines about how he never hits the flop with A, Q. Let him know that you got lucky and hit two pair on the turn. Congratulate him on laying down A, Q before it cost him a lot of money. Never mind that if he had raised pre-flop, you never would have called. Let him think he is just suffering some bad luck. You are in control. Opponents are afraid to raise you. Keep them that way. Dictate the terms of play in a diplomatic fashion.

How far you take your diplomacy is up to your own comfort level. I recently was playing in a $200 buy-in no limit hold'em tournament. There were unlimited rebuys in the first hour of play so long as you were even or down in chips. The player to my immediate left was late in getting to his seat and missed about one round of play. Well, he made up for lost time in a hurry. To say this player (let us call him Player X) was horrible was an understatement. At one point, Player X raised $500 in chips pre-flop and had one caller who went all-in for $550. It was only another $50 for Player X to call, and he had approximately another $500 in chips. To everyone's surprise, Player X folded. Even the player who had won the hand looked confused and asked what just happened. Player X responded in a curt tone that he was re-raised and he folded.

No one questioned his play or pointed out the complete folly of his fold. Player X went through his initial stack and three more (at a total cost of $800) in less than half an hour. At that point, he finally gave up. As bad as Player X was, he certainly was not going to get any sympathy from anyone at the table. During the short time he played, Player X managed to insult just about everyone's play at the table with absolutely no hint of irony. Every time Player X re-bought, he reached into his pocket and pulled out a stack of $100 bills the size of his fist. I have no idea where he got his bankroll, but it certainly was not from playing poker. As rude and obnoxious as Player X was, no one at the table dared talk back to him. Not out of fear of retribution, mind you. Rather, everyone was content to let Player X enrich everyone else at the table. His unpleasantness was a small price to pay. I think everyone at the table handled Player X extremely well. No one was rattled by Player X's rudeness, and everyone who had the chance took advantage of his poor play. I would say that everyone handled Player X with diplomacy.

Then, about five minutes after Player X first sat down, a player (let us call him Player Y) not in the tournament who obviously knew Player X approached the table. Player Y put his hand on Player X's shoulder and pleaded with him to come back to the Omaha hi-lo ring game that he had been playing. Player X responded that he was in the middle of a tournament and that he would return once he was eliminated or had won the whole thing. Player Y would not take no for an answer. Player Y tried to convince Player X that the real action was back at the Omaha table and that he should just walk away from the tournament. Obviously, Player X's Omaha play was no better than his no limit hold'em play. To his credit, Player X did not leave immediately.

Now, I am all for being diplomatic at the poker table. However, once a player leaves the table, I am not comfortable chasing after a player to come back. Player Y was practicing diplomacy to the nth degree, although I think most players would agree that he crossed the line.

Politics

Poker is a great study in small group dynamics. You are playing in close proximity with up to nine other players. Each player has his own goal that is in direct conflict with the goals of everyone else at the table. The poker table is a political arena with all the players aiming for the same position. To maximize success requires some political skill. You must outmaneuver your opponents without inspiring their backlash; become the leader through skill and cunning. Part of that cunning is to keep the players in line. When you are the leader, it will be much easier to enforce your rules if the players are content. Machiavelli recognized that even the most ruthless of rules are likely to be accepted if there is a feeling of common good among the people. Certainly, you do not want to share your chips with the other players. However, there are other ways to make the players feel good about their play even if they are losing.

People play poker for a number of reasons. Most people play for recreational purposes. Poker affords them the opportunity to indulge their competitive spirit at the same time they are having a good time. While, certainly, every player wants to win, most casual players will not judge the quality of time spent at the poker table by how much they win or lose. Rather, if they had a good time, made some decent plays, and won a few pots, they will feel satisfied. Poker is the perfect game for people to internalize. It is human nature to believe we are responsible for our successes through our skill and fortitude. When we suffer defeats, we are quick to make excuses. Poker, with the capriciousness of Fortune inherent in every hand, offers everyone a ready-made excuse. Win and you are a heckuva player. Lose and you are unlucky.

Be a politician. Maintain a player-friendly table even while you are seeking to maximize your profits from these very players. Many a player has walked away from a table down some money yet satisfied. They are convinced that they played well and have a few winning pots to support their conviction. Furthermore, they truly believe that if they just had a little luck they would have been up. Surely, they tell themselves, things will even out next time and Fortune will smile on them.

Reinforce those feelings in your opponents. Most of us have strong negative feelings toward modern-day politicians. We find them disingenuous and unworthy of our trust. Everyone knows people at work who are getting ahead not because they deserve it but because they are politicians. While most of us would be uncomfortable getting ahead this way, the poker room is a different arena. Behavior that would be unacceptable to you in your private life or in the corporate world is perfectly acceptable when you sit down at the poker table. How you attain success at poker is completely divorced from your private morality. Adopt a different mindset when you enter the poker room. Be a politician, and check your old self at the door. He will still be there when you leave.

Tactical Strategy

Every great statesman throughout history has been a master of tactical strategy. One can ascend to leadership by possessing keen diplomatic and political skills, but if that leader fails to grasp and implement strategy, he will ultimately fail. The possession of diplomatic and political skills will be immensely important in carrying out your proposed tactical strategy. However, no diplomatic and political skill in the world will compensate for the absence of an insightful tactical strategy.

To be a successful poker player requires a tremendous amount of base knowledge. Before you sit down to any poker game, you should know how to calculate the odds of your hand against what your opponent is likely to have. You do not need to know the exact odds, but the approximate calculation for most situations should be secondhand knowledge. For instance, if you are playing hold'em with a low pair pre-flop, you should not even have to think to know that you are a heavy underdog heads-up against a higher pair or that you have an approximately 50 percent chance heads-up against two overcards.

Assuming each player comes to the table with a firm understanding of the fundamentals, then the player who will be successful is the one who can out-strategize his opponents. This will be the player who mixes up his play. This will be the player who knows his opponents and has the foresight to think one or two moves ahead of them. This will be the player who understands the consequences of all his potential actions. This is the player who will understand all the factors comprising the situation. This is the player who adapts to the ever-changing circumstances and environment.

Before you sit down to the table to play any game, you need to know the fundamentals of that game cold. Once you sit down, however, do not always play by the book. Do not blindly play your cards. Play the situation every time it is your turn to act. Experiment to find a style and strategy that you are comfortable implementing and that you are successful with. Remember that your poker game should be forever evolving. Strive to improve consistently and mix up your play in order to stay ahead of the competition.

Against inferior competition, a thorough knowledge of the game and odds you are playing will provide you with an inherent advantage. You can play relatively straightforward and exploit your opponent's lack of knowledge. However, as you move up to better competition, you must adjust. Your opponents will have the same understanding of the game as you do. They will be anticipating your hands and moves and will be doing everything in their power to get you to make mistakes. You must mix up your play to keep them from getting a read on you. You must keep your play unpredictable while still maintaining your discipline. To accomplish this, you must know your opponent. You must know how he plays, but you must also know how he perceives your play. An astute opponent will force you to try more unorthodox moves.

On occasion, you should play a marginal hand with strength against an astute opponent. You may still want to reveal your hand even if you force your opponent to fold. For instance, if you find that an opponent seems to be making all the right moves against you, wait for a situation to get heads-up with him and do something unorthodox. Play a marginal hand with strength. Win or lose, you may want to reveal your hand. Good players take great pride in ascertaining what hands their opponents hold. When they guess wrong, this can undermine their confidence. As you erode their confidence, you will soon find them not making all the right moves against you.

Geography

In warfare, a thorough understanding of the geographical features of the contested area is critical to military success. A good leader will become learned in the description, distribution, and interaction of the diverse physical, biological, and cultural features of the contested earth. Likewise, in poker the good player will study and analyze the relative strengths and weaknesses of each player at the table: how the players interact with each other and how each player's position affects the overall flow of the game.

A good poker player must be pragmatic and proactive. He must create an edge for himself whenever and wherever he can find it. He must scrutinize every aspect of the game. The successful poker player must be a good tactician. In order to be a good tactician, you must analyze the geography of the poker table the same way a general would analyze the geography of the area of battle.

Know where the trouble spots are. Avoid the loose aggressive player unless you have a strong hand. Test the unpredictable player to get a read on him. Know how the wild player plays, not only against you, but against other players. Be aware of how much money each player has and what it means to him. Know who is playing scared and who is on tilt.

Certain players will feel intimidated by some players but not others. Know the dynamics of each relationship at the table so that you can use it to your advantage. Say you are in a pot with Players A and B, and you would like to win the pot right now. You know Player A is likely to fold to a bet by Player B but not necessarily a bet by you. If you are first to act and Player B is second, check to Player B if you know him to be an aggressive player. Once Player B bets, causing Player A to fold, you can now check-raise with a good chance of forcing Player B out if he was trying to steal the pot.

Piggyback off your opponents. Say you are in a three-way pot with Players A and B. You are first to act followed in order by Player A and B. Player A is very aggressive, but you are not worried about his hand for you know he is on a draw. However, you think Player B may have you beat with his medium-strength hand. Bet out if you think Player A will raise, causing Player B to fold. Use Player A to put pressure on Player B. Player B may call one bet but not two. Understand the geography of the table so you can exploit it to your advantage.

See how each player plays in each situation. Find out if your opponents are sophisticated enough to mix up their play consistently and to adjust to the ever-changing circumstances. A move that may work against an opponent heads-up may not work against the same opponent in a multiway pot.

Know what circumstances you are playing in. Do not chase drawing hands when you are heads-up. Play drawing hands in multiway pots when it is inexpensive to do so. Play each hand according to the quality of players, the number of players, and the position of the players for that hand. If you are playing seven card stud, you must be prepared for the position to change with each new card. Anticipate how the position could change and what you can do to take advantage of any change in position. For example, you may want to raise with a semi-bluffing hand in late position if it is likely you may be in early position the next round. If you do get to bet from early position the next round, you may be able to win the pot with a strong bet on the heels of your previous raise. For example, say the player to your left is forced to open with the 2♣ up. A player with an 8♦ up calls as well as a player with the 9♥ up. You are last to act, and you decide to raise with your 9♦, 10♣ down and K♦ up. You know it is highly likely that you will be first to act for the next couple of rounds. If your opponents are playing cards or a medium pair, you stand an excellent chance of winning the pot if they do not improve. It does not matter whether you improve. Betting out of first position will put your opponents on the defensive and make it difficult for them to call with hands that get weaker with each card.

In poker, remain aware of how quickly the geographical conditions can change. Players can tighten up or go on tilt. Players change seats, money changes hands, and players come and go taking and bringing money with them. You must take note of every change and be aware of and how each such change will affect the overall play and the play of each player at the table.

History

The successful poker player will have an appreciation for the importance of history in the game. To take advantage of poker history, one must study and analyze not only his own play but that of his opponents. While you will make many mistakes on your own, you will not play enough to make them all. Poker is a game of infinite possibilities. So learn from everyone's play.

Every time you play with someone, notice how he plays. Even in hands you fold, stay engaged. Try to figure out what hands your opponents are likely to be playing. Decide how you would have played the same hand. Compare and contrast styles. Become a student of the game. Talk to other players. Take advantage of poker chat rooms and message boards to discuss various scenarios and hand histories. Get other perspectives. After every poker session you participate in, take time to reflect on your play. Analyze what you did right as well as what you did wrong. Ask yourself how you can improve and what you can learn from your opponents' play. So long as you are playing poker, you should be striving for ways to improve your play and outwit your opponents.

Poker is a game of strategy, fortune, position, and psychology. A strong historical perspective of your play and the play of your opponents will provide you with an edge in each of these aspects of the game. You must constantly aim to improve all aspects of your game so that you can stay ahead of your opponents. Staying on top of your game is the only way to defeat the toughest opponent of all—human nature.

VIII

Human Nature

Prevalent throughout Machiavelli's writings is a realist's view of human nature. He asserted that people are generally self-interested. However, Machiavelli found that people were generally content so long as they did not feel that they were victims of a horrible injustice. In the face of adversity, though, people are likely to appeal to their most selfish desires. When people are in a desperate situation, they will resort to deceit in order to turn a profit.

While Machiavelli found that the leaders of society possessed the same inherent traits as the common mass of people, he recognized the presence of one overriding trait in the few who came to lead that the common mass of people did not possess—ambition. Machiavelli found that most common people are satisfied with the status quo, while leaders strive for something more. That something more is power.

Machiavelli developed his view of human nature in the context of society at large and applied it to the political power struggles inherent in society during his time. While the poker tables of the twenty-first century are a long way away from Renaissance Italy, human nature has not changed. Machiavelli's view of human nature is as applicable today as it was then and it has particular relevance to the trenches of the poker room.

What kind of person are you?

The first question every potential poker player should ask himself before sitting down to the table is what kind of person am I. Specifically, am I a leader or one of the masses? Am I content with the status quo, or do I strive for more? Am I ambitious? If so, how ambitious am I?

In poker, as in life, there will be leaders and those who are content with the status quo. However, poker is a highly competitive contest. Thus, the percentage of players possessing high ambitions will be larger than a random sampling of society. If you are not a competitive, ambitious person, you will have a difficult time succeeding at poker over the long run. If you are content with the status quo, you can still play poker and enjoy it immensely. Poker can serve as an excellent break from the rigors of everyday schedules. Just be sure to play within your means and do not let losses upset you. If you play within your means, view playing as cheap entertainment where it does not matter if you win or lose.

If, on the other hand, you are highly ambitious, the poker room is a great place to satisfy your competitive "jones." In just about every poker room, you should be able to find a game at every skill level. To find the appropriate game for you requires an honest assessment of your own overall skill and temperament. The ideal game is a table you can control and lead. You want to dictate the terms of play in order to be successful. Find a table that you can afford with players whose ambitions may be something less than yours maybe.

Above all else, you must be honest with yourself. If you are consistently losing, examine your play. Everyone will suffer bad beats and losing streaks. That is poker. However, a steady string of losses most likely signifies a more fundamental underlying problem. Are you playing too many hands? Are you playing too tight? Are you being outplayed? Ask yourself these questions and answer them honestly. Poker is a game of ready-made excuses. It is human nature to credit your winnings to skill and your losses to bad luck. Do not fall into that trap. Every player has had to start somewhere. Everyone who has played the game has had his moments when the game and the opponents got the best of him. What distinguishes winning players, however, is their ability to recognize their shortcomings and then work like heck to improve.

Do not delude yourself about your play. Ignoring the problems in your play will only lead to further losses and prevent you from improving. Get to know your skill level, your limitations, and your potential so that you can work to improve your optimal level of play. Ask yourself, am I a leader? If not, can I transform myself into one?

Examine your play honestly. Do you play your opponents or just your cards? Do you look for opportunities to exploit? Do you have a hard time laying down strong but losing hands? Are you consistently adjusting to the ever-changing circumstances at the poker table? Do you mix up your play to keep your opponents from getting a read on you? Do you check and call a lot, or do you bet and raise when you are in hands? Are you passive or aggressive? The answers to these questions will help you determine whether you possess leadership qualities at the poker table. If you do not, ask yourself whether you are capable and willing to do what it takes to make yourself a leader and a winner at the table.

How to play against the masses.

How do you play against the common masses? The accepted school of thought in most poker literature is if you play against inferior opponents, you just outplay them. You do not get fancy, and you just play fundamentally sound poker. While that is solid advice, it ignores the psychological component of the game. Remember Machiavelli's teachings of what inspires the masses. Most people are content with the status quo unless they feel they have suffered a horrible injustice. Eventually, every poker player will feel he has suffered a horrible injustice at the table. Thus, it is the whim of Fortune.

A player who believes he has just taken a tough beat will become a dangerous player. While he will ultimately do more harm to himself than anyone else if he lets his emotions get the best of him, in the interim he will be dangerous because his play may become more wild and unpredictable. Conversely, that player may become more dangerous because he may get better. Losing has different effects on different people. Understanding the makeup of your opponent will go a long way in determining how he is likely to respond to adversity. Once you have that understanding, you can adjust your play accordingly and retain your edge.

Keep in mind that a player who is losing a lot of money or feels that he is suffering horrible luck is likely to undergo an attitude adjustment. This player will not be content with the status quo. He will have his back against the wall, and his instinctual desire to fight back will kick in. How he fights back and your ability to recognize it will go a long way in determining your ultimate success. Does this player buckle down and play better, or does he go on tilt? Does this player tighten up and play scared? Know your opponent and know the situation so that you can consistently adapt your play to the nuances of the game. An understanding of your opponent's nature will help you anticipate his play especially during those times when predictable aspects of human nature are sure to take over.

The key to being a successful leader at the poker table is to control the table while keeping the masses happy. Do not let them feel victimized. Compliment and encourage their play. If they suffer a bad beat, keep their spirits up. Let them know that there is a lot of luck in poker and that theirs is sure to turn around soon.

Your opponents should know, however, that you are the leader. That should be their status quo. When they make mistakes, punish them quickly and consistently. Exploit their weaknesses. Machiavelli believed that fear is a more compelling emotion than love. It bears repeating, as a leader, it is far preferable to be feared than loved. It is best to be feared and respected, but not hated. To keep the masses content while maintaining a healthy level of fear is a delicate balancing act for a leader to perform. As hard as it is to do in the political arena, it is exponentially harder at the poker table where your goal is to take your opponent's chips directly from him.

How do you accomplish this? Play your game and take what you want, not just what your opponents give you. Mix up your play to keep it unpredictable. Never reveal more information than you have to. Study your opponents and the situation. Test your opponents to gather information. Be respectful of your opponents. Show them respect, not just in your demeanor, but in your play. For instance, say you are playing hold'em and you are heads-up with a weak opponent after the flop. Your opponent raised under the gun, and you called in the big blind with J, 10 suited. The flop comes 4, 5, 9 rainbow. You are confident that the flop did not help your opponent, so you make a bet to try to steal the pot. Your opponent raises. Now, you have an easy lay down. However, rather than throw your hand away immediately, take some time. Throwing your hand away that fast instantly sends a clear signal to your opponent that you thought you could steal the pot from him. Take your time, and when you finally fold, say something like, "I think your pair is better than mine." Give your opponent credit for a hand. Show him respect. This will accomplish two things: it will keep him happy with the status quo, and it will keep your true intentions in that hand well hidden. This will allow you to attempt a similar move later without prejudice.

Everything you do at the poker table should be to maximize profits. Opponents who are content with the status quo are ideal opponents. However, to maximize your profits requires more than just outplaying them. You must study and understand their nature and know how they are likely to react in the face of adversity so that you may properly handle them as well as maximize your profits.

If you are playing with weak players, be the first to act. There is a great advantage in being the first to bet. You project strength and leadership. So long as you are playing discriminately, your opponents must respect your bet. When you bet out, you put your opponent on the defensive and force him to make a decision. If he folds, your bet has paid off. If he calls or raises, it should give you a good indication as to the strength of his hand.

Do not take unnecessary chances against an inferior player. This is a common mistake of even the most experienced of players. Do not risk a ton of chips heads-up against a weak opponent, even though you are a slight favorite. While this would be the proper play against a good player, it is poor strategy against a poor player for one simple reason: you are highly likely to find yourself in much more favorable situations against the poor player. Wait for him to bet a lot of chips.

For example, say you are playing no limit hold'em and you are in the big blind with K♠, 2♠. A weak player makes a medium raise (you put him on a pair of tens), and everyone folds to you. You call to defend your blind, and also because you are confident, you can outplay the weak player after the flop. The flop comes 8♠, 3♠, 2♥. Even though you are behind in the hand, you are actually a slight favorite to win with your one pair and a flush draw. You act first and decide to go all-in. You hope to win the pot right there, but even if you are called, you are a slight favorite if you are correct in putting your opponent on a pair of tens. Your opponent calls and turns over his pair of tens. The turn and river bring no help and you lose the pot.

Now, if you were playing against a strong opponent, you could feel good about this play, even though you lost. In the end, you will make money being all-in with a hand that is a favorite to win. Since the opportunities to beat a strong opponent will be scarce, you must take advantage of every one of them if you are going to succeed.

However, against a weak opponent, the opportunities to defeat him will be plentiful. So why risk a lot when you are only a slight favorite? You are leaving much too much to chance. Wait until you are a heavy favorite to get him all-in. That opportunity is sure to come. In the interim, you can slowly hack away at his chip stack by exploiting his weaknesses.

While you certainly should be able to outplay a weak opponent, you must always understand your particular opponent. For example, many weak players just play their cards blindly and do not pay attention to their opponents. If you are up against a table of these players, you do not need to mix up your play as much as you normally would since it would largely go unnoticed. Many weak players will stick with a decent starting hand until the river no matter what. Say you are playing $5–$10 seven card stud and your weak opponent starts with a pair of Jacks that you know he will play until the end no matter what. You start with K♣, Q♣ (down) and 9♣ (up). Your opponent bets $5 and you call. On fourth street you receive 10♣ and your opponent draws a blank. Again, your opponent bets $5 and you call. On fifth street you catch the ace of spades and your opponent catches another blank. Even though you are behind, you have very scary up cards.

Against a decent opponent, you may want to check-raise here. A check-raise attempt here is a good move for a couple of reasons: First, if you check, your opponent may not bet if he senses a trap, and, thus, you get a free card to your drawing hand. Second, if your opponent does bet out, then when you raise, he may very well believe he is beat and fold. Finally, even if he does not fold, another scary card on sixth street (such as a fourth spade) is sure to chase him out. However, this move is wasted against an opponent who will stay with those tens to the river. Against this opponent, you would just want to check and hope you get a free card. You would not want to check-raise until you improved to a better hand than his.

How do you play against ambitious players?

The first step is to identify an ambitious player. An ambitious player will mix up his game effectively, implement deception strategically, exploit his opponents' weaknesses, and punish the mistakes of others. An ambitious player will know his opponents and the situation so that he may take advantage of any potential opportunity. An ambitious player will attempt to take what he wants, not just what his opponent gives him. In short, an ambitious player will be doing everything that you should be doing to maximize profits.

Since the ambitious player will be mixing up his play, it will take more time and effort to get a read on him. This is the kind of player who you will want to test to see how he reacts. Raise him when you think he is on a steal. Call even though you think he has you beat if you can gain some valuable information. Ask to see his cards when he mucks a showdown.

When playing an ambitious opponent, you must do all the things you otherwise would do in order to be the leader of the table. You must put every attribute of virtu to work for you. In addition, you will have to implement other things in order to gain valuable information about the ambitious opponent and to keep him from gaining too much insight into your play. Try more unorthodox plays on the ambitious player. Project a wilder image to him. Let him think you are out of control when in fact you are playing a very disciplined game. To accomplish this, you may want to reveal cards purposely even when you do not have to. While this is contrary to your overall plan of revealing as little information as possible, you can reveal cards to your advantage. If you chase him off a pot with nothing, turn over your cards. While this is not a tactic you want to use against a less ambitious opponent, in this instance you have more to gain from projecting a wild image than worrying about showing your opponent a lot of respect.

With an ambitious opponent, your top priority is to establish your dominance. If he fears you, he will be unable to control his play. His judgment will be impaired out of apprehensiveness as to what you may do. In order to make him fear you, you must be able to anticipate his play and adjust yours accordingly. You must outwit him while avoiding falling victim to his advanced play.

While a nonambitious player will occasionally attempt to steal a pot, this player will typically give up if not successful the first time. An ambitious player, on the other hand, will not only attempt to steal a pot on third street but will try again on fourth and fifth street as well if he feels his opponent is vulnerable. He will not give up. In addition, an ambitious player will attempt to induce bluffs on the river. To induce a bluff on the river, a player must check his last opportunity to make a bet. This move takes a lot of guts, because if it is not successful, a player has lost his last chance to bet with a winning hand. However, if successful, the player will win two bets instead of one. This is a move only ambitious players will attempt.

You must avoid mistakes against an ambitious opponent. While you can often get away with mistakes against a weak opponent (or at least recover from them), an ambitious player will make you pay dearly for your mistakes. In a game with highly skilled opponents, the difference between winning and losing is often one hand an hour. That is, the loser will make about one mistake an hour on average that the winner will exploit. The mistake may be as obvious as folding a winning hand, or it could be as subtle as not doing everything you could to maximize your profits when you had a strong hand. The subtle mistakes are the more common, and often more costly. They are the mistakes strong players make when they are up against an ambitious opponent. While you should always respect your opponents' play and abilities, be careful not to give them more credit than they deserve. Tough, ambitious opponents will win hands against you and outmaneuver you on occasion. They will also get cards against you. Do not let these things throw you off your game. When you give them too much credit, you tighten up and play scared. Remember that they are playing with the same deck as you are. They cannot have good cards all the time. Choose your battles carefully with ambitious opponents, but do not be afraid to engage them in battle.

Against an ambitious opponent, you must employ a complete Machiavellian strategy. Your ambitious opponent is your chief rival to everything you want at the poker table. He wants to dictate the terms of play. He wants to maximize his profits. He wants to ascend to the leadership of the table. He wants you to fear him. He will do everything necessary to accomplish his goals. He knows that there is only one way to be judged at the poker table: *si guarda al fine*.

To combat this ambitious opponent requires a totally focused campaign. You must treat him as the enemy to be defeated at all costs. You must use any means necessary. You must have an understanding of Machiavelli's *Art of War*.

IX.

The Art of War

While *The Prince* is Machiavelli's most widely read treatise, Machiavelli was the author of many works including a collection entitled *The Books on the Art of War*. The prevalent theme throughout this collection is one that is highly applicable to the poker table. Machiavelli recognized that many scholars of his day believed that nothing could be more dissimilar than military life is from civilian life. The mentality, discipline, and readiness necessary for military life were vastly different from what was needed in civilian life. However, Machiavelli saw a common thread in all disciplines of life. He believed if civilians in other institutions adopted the traits necessary for military success, they would ultimately prove successful as well.

When men enter the military, Machiavelli observed, they quickly change their clothes, customs, habits, and voice. This was necessary in order for a soldier to be quick and ready for any violence. Civilian customs and habits are not conducive to military actions. In particular, a man with civilian customs would be hard-pressed to make other men afraid. Machiavelli believed that in order to build the foundation of a solid civilian society, as in the military, it was necessary for the people to live in fear of the laws of that society.

How does all of this adapt to the poker table? While recognizing that in no way, shape, or form does poker approach the level of somberness of war, there are numerous tenets that can be distilled from *The Books on the Art of War* that can be applied to poker. Chief among these are as follows:

- Adopt a military mind-set.
- Defend and protect your assets.
- Plan ahead, and you will be led to victory.
- Disrupt an opposing force with the element of surprise.
- Make the people live in fear of your laws.

Adopt a military mind-set.

When you enter the poker room, check your civilian mind-set at the door. Your customs and habits should be radically different from your everyday life. Adopt the mind-set of a general in the heat of battle. You want to instill fear in your opponents and defeat the enemy. You cannot be concerned with things that would make a difference in polite society.

You are seated at a poker table, and you are expected to use cunning, guile, and skill to win. To play with anything less than your best will greatly hurt your profits and will also deprive your opponents of the competition they expect.

Do whatever is necessary to put yourself in the right mind-set. If wearing different clothes than you normally would helps shed your civilian self, do it. If wearing headsets and listening to music helps you focus, do it. If working out before you play makes you feel stronger, do it. If drinking a cup of coffee gives you an extra sense of awareness, do it. Do whatever you need to do to psyche yourself up and to lose any moral reservations that are only applicable in your civilian life.

Too many beginning poker players take self-defeating positions. They are afraid to bluff because they are afraid to get caught. The potential embarrassment they will suffer is too much to bear. This is a loser's mentality. Think about it. What is the worst thing that can happen if you bluff? You get caught. In that case, you congratulate your opponent on the nice call, and you have now made your play less predictable to every other player at the table. This will only help you get paid later when you do make a hand. On the other hand, your bluff may work. In which case, you will win a pot you otherwise would not have, and your opponents will never be quite sure if you were bluffing or not.

So what is there to be embarrassed about? Absolutely nothing if you have a military mind-set. Generals think many steps ahead and take calculated risks. They know they may lose a few battles, but they are only concerned with winning the war. They care not the least about their opponents' feelings. They only care about winning. In order to accomplish that, they must deceive and trap their opponent. The rules of war offer few constraints.

The playing field in civilian life is vastly different. There are legal, ethical, and moral boundaries in which we all must live and follow in order to maintain a structured society. There are very few arenas in which it is acceptable to deceive and trap an opponent. Since deception is fundamentally wrong, we naturally (and rightfully) feel guilty about employing it in everyday life. If you do not check your civilian attitude at the door of the poker room, these feelings will carry over to your play, and you will be incapable of playing your best.

Modern society places a great deal of emphasis on winning. We tend to look only at short-term results, and we are quick to classify both teams and individuals as winners or losers. Thus, we have been trained to be embarrassed to lose. One's success in poker, however, must be measured over the long term.

Every poker player is going to lose many hands in his lifetime. Too many beginning players are afraid to lose. This is a self-defeating proposition. Again, these players bring their civilian attitudes with them. They are not looking at the big picture. They do not have the mind-set of a general. If a general were afraid to lose a battle, he would never win a war.

There are many times in poker when you should see a showdown, even though you know you are going to lose. That is right. There are many times in poker when you should see a showdown, even though you are fairly sure you have the *worst of it*. For instance, if you are getting pot odds to call, you should call. That is, if you have a one-in-ten chance of winning but are getting twenty-to-one odds to call, by all means call. So long as you win your expected 10 percent of the time in these situations, you will be making money. There are other times when you should call to let your opponents know that you cannot easily be chased away.

I see a great number of beginning players chase hands only to fold consistently on the river when they do not complete their hand. More experienced players will pick up on this right away and take advantage. They will bet on the river with nothing, knowing the beginning player will fold. However, the beginning player will continue to fold because he is too embarrassed to turn over a losing hand. He does not want to see a showdown unless he has a sure winner.

If you are going to play poker, you cannot fear losing hands. Your only goal is to win money over the long term. In order to accomplish that, you must be willing to probe and test your opponents and take chances. This will necessitate losing some hands along the way. That is the cost of playing poker.

There are a lot of paradoxes in poker. One of the most important to remember is that while you are expected to be civil at the table, you must not bring your civilian customs and habits to the table. You want to exercise every aspect of virtu. You want to become the leader of the table. You want to intimidate your opponents with your play. Most importantly, you must be prepared to attack at all times. When you see an opportunity, you must exploit it. You must be on edge in order to gain an edge.

Civilians are not trained to attack. Military men are. In poker, your chips are your force. You must be prepared to engage them at all times. You attack by betting into and raising your opponents. Your opponents are your enemy on the battlefield. You cannot be worried about offending them or hurting their feelings as you would in the civilian world.

This does not mean that you should be on the offensive at all times. In fact, you should engage your chips judiciously. Do not needlessly squander your force. While you will only attack at opportune times, however, you must be prepared to attack at all times. Only with such preparedness will you be able to act when the time is right.

Defend and protect your assets.

Successful generals know the importance of defending their positions and protecting their men. They do not risk lives unless necessary or give up ground to the enemy. In order to win the war, they know that they must live to fight another day.

In poker, the chips that you do not lose are just as important as the chips that you win. Do not needlessly put your chips at risk. Your chips are your force. They are weapons to employ when they can exert the most damage. It is typically better to make one raise than two calls. It is typically better to bet out than to check and call. When you do use your chips, you want to be the aggressor. There will, of course, be exceptions. For instance, if you are calling when you have pot odds, you are trying to find out information or you have a good drawing hand in a multiway pot.

Overall, you need to have a military mind-set. Do not think of your chips as a commodity that you can easily buy more of by reaching into your pocket and opening up your wallet. Remember that your chips are your force. When properly engaged, they can be very powerful. When used to strike at the right times, you will make money. If squandered needlessly, you will have wasted a valuable asset. Make your chips work for you.

If you play from strength rather than from weakness, then you impose your will on your opponent and you have the advantage. For example, say you are in the big blind with 7♣, 8♥ and you have one caller before the flop. The flop comes 5♦, 8♦, 9♠. Unbeknownst to you, your opponent has Q♠, J♠, giving him a *gut shot* straight draw and two overcards. If you bet out first, your opponent will put you on a better hand, and depending on the circumstances, he may or may not call, as he does have a number of outs. If the turn brings him no help and you continue to bet, it becomes more difficult for him to call. Finally, if the river brings no help and you continue to bet out, he has no choice but to fold (or try a risky bluff raise). By betting out, you have kept him on the defensive, and he must decide each time whether to fold or pay for the opportunity to draw out.

Now, suppose that after the flop, instead of betting, you decide that with a *middle pair* and a gut shot straight draw you have a playable hand, but perhaps not the strongest, so you check. Your opponent immediately bets and now you are on the defensive. You have to be the one to decide if it is worth calling or if your opponent has a better hand. Even if in both hypotheticals the amount of money bet is identical, you are in a vastly superior position in the first scenario where you bet out first. You stand a much greater chance of winning the pot if your opponent does not draw out. In the second scenario, you will face some very difficult decisions if you do not improve. If a scare card such as an ace or a third diamond falls on the turn, you will probably have to fold in the face of a bet from your opponent, even though it does not help him.

The biggest difference in these two scenarios is that in the first one you are using your chips as force. You are being the aggressor and putting your opponent on the defensive. In the second scenario, you are using your chips as currency to buy another card. Even though the amount you are betting is the same in both scenarios, you stand a much greater chance of winning when you play with strength and use your chips as force.

Plan ahead, and you will be led to victory.

Poker is a battle of wits. It is a game that requires a great deal of knowledge and a great deal of skill in order to be successful. It is a game of infinite possibilities and a game of imperfect information. It is a game that requires you to make quick decisions that can make or cost you a lot of money.

How do you put yourself in a position to make the right decisions when you have limited information? The answer is in your preparation. Poker is a game of never-ending preparation. The learning curve never ends, and each opponent and situation is unique.

The preparation should begin way before you sit down at the poker table. A comprehensive knowledge of the fundamentals of the game you will be playing is necessary. You should know what is, and what is not, a playable hand in every situation. You should know how to determine pot odds for every situation. You should know in which situations to check, bet, raise, or call. Understanding these concepts only gives you a base knowledge that you can assume every other player will know as well. What comes next is what separates winning players from losing ones. First, you must adopt the proper mind-set. You need to shed your civilian self and adopt your warrior persona that embodies all the elements of virtù.

Once you know the fundamentals, you can experiment with breaking them. If you do everything by the book, your play will be predictable. You must learn how to exploit opportunities, punish your opponents' mistakes, and attack your opponents' vulnerabilities.

To accomplish this, you must, at all times, pay strict attention to the action at the table. You cannot be distracted. You must study every player.

You must notice every factor and observe how those factors are ever-changing. Pay attention to who is up and who is down and how that is af-fecting their game. Take note if someone leaves the table and someone else arrives. If you are playing stud, take the time to study each card as it comes out. In stud, you should always look at your card(s) last. You want to capture the look on each player's face as he sees his cards. In addition, you want to see their cards in case they fold quickly. Your cards are not going anywhere, so do not be in a hurry to look at them.

Know your opponent and know yourself. Know your limitations and know what you are capable of. If you try a move you are not comfortable making, you are sure to give a tell. Play within your game. If you stay within your game, then you can gain an edge by understanding your opponent's play. Study your opponent. Test him to get a read on him. Put him on the defensive. Bet into him, or check-raise him, to see how he re-acts. The difference between winning and losing in a competitive game is about one well-played hand an hour. That is, the winner will exploit one mistake an hour or avoid making that one mistake an hour or will get a lucky hand once during the hour. Since the lucky hands will even out over the long run, the player who can avoid mistakes while exploiting his opponents' vulnerabilities will be successful.

The difference between winning and losing in poker is a very fine line. The most prepared player will be the one on the right side of that line. That will be the player who is prepared to handle adversity and the whims of Fortune. That will be the player who knows the fundamentals and knows how to mix up his play. That will be the player who remains aware of every factor comprising the current situation and can anticipate how those factors will be changing. That will be the player who knows himself and knows his opponent so that he can use his strengths to outwit his opponent.

Disrupt an opposing force with the element of surprise.

In order to outwit your opponent, you must anticipate your opponent's play while keeping your play unpredictable. Certainly, anticipating your opponent's play begins with observation. But how do you keep your opponent's play predictable once you engage him? The best way is to play hands only with strength. When you play hands discriminately and with strength, you put your opponent on the defensive. Anytime a player is on the defensive, his play is likely to be more predictable. He is forced to make a decision, and his response is likely to be very revealing.

If putting your opponent on the defensive helps keep his play predictable, it follows that your play will be predictable if you allow your opponent to put you on the defensive. Do not play passively. Try to avoid calling bets unless you are on a draw in a multiway pot and you are getting sufficient pot odds to do so. Re-raise overly aggressive opponents to curb their betting. Finally, you must mix up your play and implement a few unorthodox moves. Look for opportune times to play marginal hands with strength. When you sense vulnerability in your opponent, attack him. Bet scare cards to project strength. When you make these unorthodox moves, stay with them. An amateur will take one shot at the pot, while an experienced player will fire at the pot all the way to the river. Do everything in your power to keep your play unpredictable. When your play is unpredictable, the element of surprise is always on your side. If your opponent cannot understand your play, he will be unable to control his own.

Make the people fear your laws.

Be the ruler. Be a Prince. Be the leader of your table. Punish your opponents' mistakes. Exploit their weaknesses. Above all else, dictate the play at your table. Make your opponents conform to you. Take what you want, not just what your opponents give you. Once you establish yourself as the leader of the table through your ability, cunning, and skill, your opponents will fear you. They will adjust their play to yours. They will be reluctant to enter pots you are in. They will be tentative in acting before it is your turn to act. When they do engage you, you will have a very good read on them since they will have made their play very predictable.

Once a player is playing scared, he can no longer control his own play and is destined to lose. Poker is a game to be played with reason and discipline but not with fear. A scared opponent will call when he should raise, fold when he should call, and check when he should bet. He will be doing things not to lose money rather than to use his chips as a force to maximize profits. Once you have effectively disengaged your opponent's force, you possess a tremendous advantage. Once disengaged, you will begin to accumulate your opponents' chips, thereby weakening them further at your expense.

X

Maxims

Prevalent throughout Machiavelli's seminal work, *The Prince*, are numerous maxims that have been studied for centuries by men and women of all walks of life. Machiavelli's advice and wisdom have stood the test of time. His view of human nature is as insightful today as it was groundbreaking at the time of its publication. Many of these maxims have particular relevance to the poker table. They are listed here.

MACHIAVELLI SAID:
[D]ominions...are acquired either by the arms of the Prince himself, or of others, or else by Fortune or by ability.

Players may gain control of the poker table through many different means. Know by which means a player has gained control. Only that player who has used his ability to gain power will be likely to remain in control. Do not be thrown off your game by someone who has ascended to power through good Fortune. Bide your time and wait for an opportunity to exploit this fraud who will lose his power as surely as he gained it.

MACHIAVELLI SAID:

[M]en change their rulers willingly, hoping to better themselves,
and this hope induces them to take up arms against him who rules.

When you gain control of the poker table, do not become complacent.
Use your power to enforce your rules and dictate play so that you can effectively shut down any attempted insurgency on the part of the other
players. Never rest on your laurels. Know that someone is waiting in the
wings to take your position the minute you let your guard down.

MACHIAVELLI SAID:

In this way, you have enemies in all those whom you have injured in
seizing that principality.

When you are successful in beating your opponents and taking their
money, they are likely to feel resentment and seek revenge. Recognize this
and use it to your advantage. Feign weakness when you sense your opponent is on tilt or overly anxious to bet into you. A revengeful opponent
will want to believe he has the better of you.

Let him think that when you have him beat.

MACHIAVELLI SAID:

[M]en ought to be well treated or crushed, because they can
avenge themselves of lighter injuries, of more serious ones they
cannot; therefore, the injury that is to be done to a man ought to
be of such a kind that one does not stand in fear of revenge.

Never take it easy on an opponent. Your goal must always be to maximize
profits and take as many chips from your opponent as you can. Whenever
you have the opportunity to cripple or bankrupt your opponent, you must
do so. If you do not take the maximum amount of chips that you can from
an opponent, you not only leave yourself weaker, but you leave your opponent stronger. This is especially true in tournament play. If you fail to
eliminate an opponent when you have the opportunity, he can come back

to beat you. Whenever you leave an opponent with more strength than you should have, you increase the possibility of him coming back to harm you.

MACHIAVELLI SAID:
[W]hen the evils that arise have been foreseen (which are only given to a wise man to see), they can quickly be redressed, but when, through not having been foreseen, they have been permitted to grow in a way that everyone can see them, there is no longer a remedy.

Always think ahead. You must stay atop the situation and anticipate how the game is changing and how the game will change. In order to outwit your opponents and gain an edge, you must prepare ahead of them. Be aware of every factor comprising the situation and take note of how those factors are likely to change. For instance, if you are playing seven card stud, position can change with every card. Do not make a bet on fourth street with an ace high in a multiway pot with the intention of leading again on fifth street. However, if you have high pair on fourth street and no one has an overcard, you are ensured of being the first to bet on fifth street. So plan accordingly.

MACHIAVELLI SAID:
The wish to acquire is in truth very natural and common. Men always do so when they can, and for this they will be praised not blamed. But when they cannot do so, yet wish to do so by any means, then there is folly and blame.

The money you save is as important as the money you win. Do not chase pots you cannot win. The single most important factor that separates winning poker players from losing ones is the ability to lay down a strong but losing hand. A winning poker player is aggressive but discriminating. He goes after what he wants when he senses an edge. When he does not sense an edge, he does not needlessly risk his chips. A losing poker player is blinded by greed and is reckless with his chips. He will chase pots against all odds.

MACHIAVELLI SAID:
[M]en, walking following in paths beaten by others, imitating their deeds, are yet unable to keep entirely to the ways of others or to attain the power of those they imitate.

There are more followers than leaders in every aspect of life. The poker room is no different. Those players who are not leaders may do well but will never do as well as the true innovators and leaders of the game. To be successful, you must take charge and try to dictate play, not follow the lead of others. Know the fundamentals of the game, but do not always play by the book.

MACHIAVELLI SAID:
A wise man ought always follow the paths beaten by great men and imitate those who have been supreme so that if his ability does not equal theirs, at least he will savor it.

All players, whether followers or leaders, can learn from the play of their opponents. Learning the art of poker is a never-ending process. As long as you are playing, you should be seeking to improve your game. You can learn a lot from your opponents—both from their mistakes and their successes. Poker is a game of infinite possibilities. No matter how much you play, you will not come close to facing every possible situation. Thus, it is critical to always pay attention and learn from the play of others. Learn everything you can (good and bad) from other players, but play in a style that is suited to you. Do not emulate others if their style does not work for you.

MACHIAVELLI SAID:
Let him act like the clever archers who, designing to hit the mark

that yet appears too far distant and knowing the limits to which the
strength of their bow attains, takes aim much higher than the mark,
not only to reach by their strength or arrow to so great a height, but
to be able, with the aid of so high an aim, to hit the mark they wish to
reach.

Poker is a game of great ambitions. You cannot play scared. In order to
maximize profits, you must realize that your opponents are your enemy.
They are there to take your money. You must defend your position while
you are simultaneously trying to conquer your enemies. Since you may
have up to nine different enemies at the poker table, you must possess
and project an abundance of confidence. Believe you are the best in order
to play to the best of your ability. Play with great confidence while maintaining your discipline. If an opponent is getting the better of you, first
determine if he is outplaying you or outdrawing you. If he is outdrawing
you, stay the course, and the chips will soon come back to you. If he is
outplaying you, then take a step back and determine a fresh way to engage him. Mix up your play and challenge him. If you are still unsuccess-
ful, take a break and perhaps try another table. Everyone who plays poker
will have sessions where no matter what they do they cannot beat a particular opponent. When that happens, cut your losses and learn from the
experience.

MACHIAVELLI SAID:
Now, as the fact of becoming a Prince from a private station pre-
supposes either ability or fortune, it is clear that one or the other
of these things will mitigate in some degree many difficulties.
Nevertheless, he who has relied least on Fortune is established the
strongest.

Never confuse skill with luck. Whether a player is performing well or
poorly, know if it is due to ability or Fortune. In addition to evaluating
your opponents, be sure to analyze your own play. You must be able to
recognize how much of a role Fortune is playing in your own winning or
losing streak. Do not give a fortuitous opponent more credit than he de-

serves. By the same token, do not allow yourself to feel invincible when Fortune is smiling on you.

MACHIAVELLI SAID (of certain great historical leaders):
These opportunities, therefore, made those men fortunate, and their superior ability enabled them to recognize the opportunity.

Success is often a result of a combination of skill and luck. If you play poker long enough, the luck will even out. Those players who capitalize on, and make the most of, their opportunities are the ones who will be successful. Luck happens when opportunity meets preparation. Know the situation at all times in order to both recognize and maximize your opportunities.

MACHIAVELLI SAID:
Those who by valiant ways become Princes acquire a principality with difficulty, but they keep it with ease.

Beware the player who becomes the leader of the table through his skill and ability especially if it comes in spite of misfortune. This player deserves your respect. Do not be intimidated by him, but do not engage him unless you clearly perceive an edge.

MACHIAVELLI SAID:
[I]t ought to be remembered that there is nothing more difficult to take in hand, more perilous to conduct, or more uncertain in its success than to take the lead in the introduction of a new order of things.

Know the fundamentals of poker but do not always play by the book. The leaders in every aspect of life are innovators. At the poker table, attempt unorthodox plays in order to mix up your play and keep your opponents off balance. Do things that your opponents will not expect. Be proactive and creative to take what you want at the poker table. To attempt unorthodox maneuvers takes courage. Do not be discouraged by others who question, or even ridicule, your play. Let them play by the book and live among the masses.

MACHIAVELLI SAID:

When [innovators] can rely on themselves and use force, then they are rarely endangered. Hence, it is that all armed prophets have conquered, and the unarmed ones have been destroyed.

The size of your chip stack is your force. Always play at a table with limits that you can easily afford. If you cannot afford to make mistakes, you cannot be innovative and you will not be successful. If you play at a table where you begin play with more chips than your opponents do, you provide yourself with a significant edge. One of the most difficult concepts for poker players to master is how to walk that fine line between chip preservation and chip accumulation. You do not want to squander your chips, but it takes chips to make chips. Specifically, you must deploy chips in order to win chips from your opponents. Experiment at lower *levels* to find that comfort zone where you are deploying your chips with force, innovation, and discrimination.

MACHIAVELLI SAID:

Those who solely by good Fortune become Princes from being private citizens have little trouble in rising, but much in keeping atop; they do have not any difficulties on the way up, because they fly, but they have many when they reach the summit.

Stay disciplined and patient when an opponent is enjoying great success due largely to good Fortune. If you keep your focus, your skill will eventually win out over the player riding a short-term wave of good Fortune.

Your goal is to win over the long term. If you remain steady in your resolve to look at the result over time and ignore the short-term fluctuations caused by Fortune, you will be successful.

> **MACHIAVELLI SAID:**
> States that rise unexpectedly, then, like all other things in nature that are born and grow rapidly, cannot leave their foundations fixed in such a way that the first storm will overthrow them; unless, as is said, those who unexpectedly become Princes are men of so much ability that they know they have to be prepared at once to hold that which Fortune has thrown into their laps, and that those foundations, which others have laid *before* they became Princes, they must lay *afterwards*.

Just because a player is enjoying short-term success due to good Fortune does not necessarily mean that he is a bad player. Fortune will smile on good players as well as bad. Study your opponent over time to see how well he plays through every situation and whim of Fortune so that you can determine how much of his success can be credited to Fortune and how much can be credited to skill.

> **MACHIAVELLI SAID:**
> For injuries ought to be done all at one time, so that, being tasted less, they offend less; benefits ought to be given little by little, so that the flavor of them may last longer.

Never show up an opponent. The beauty of bluffing in poker is that if it is successful, your opponent will never know. If you win with a better hand than your opponent has, your opponent will not be offended. The only time your opponent will know he has been outplayed is in a situation in which you slow play a winning hand in order to induce your opponent to bet into you. When you have the opportunity to do this, by all means do so to maximize your profits. Most opponents will congratulate you on this play for one simple reason. They would greatly prefer to believe that you played the hand extremely well rather than believe that they played it poorly.

Whenever your opponent beats you, compliment his play. When your opponent makes a big bet and you have absolute garbage, take your time in folding. When you finally do fold, let your opponent think his tough play was the cause of your fold. Provide your opponent with false confidence.

> **MACHIAVELLI SAID:**
> A Prince can never secure himself against a hostile people.

The object of poker is to win money not to impress opponents or make enemies. Poker is a game of deception. Part of that deception is keeping your opponents engaged, friendly, and nonhostile at the table even while you are taking their money. You want opponents to respect and fear you but not resent you.

> **MACHIAVELLI SAID:**
> The worst that a Prince may expect from a hostile people is to be abandoned by them, but from hostile nobles, he has not only to fear abandonment but also to fear that they will rise up against him. For they, being in these affairs makes them more farseeing and astute.

By being hostile or creating a hostile environment, you risk having the weak players leave the table. These are the very people you want to encourage to play. However, what is worse is that the good players will rise to the occasion to challenge you at every opportunity.

> **MACHIAVELLI SAID:**
> A Prince who can command, and is a man of courage, undismayed in adversity, who does not fail in other qualifications and who, by his resolution and energy, keeps the whole people encouraged is one who will never find himself deceived by them.

Gain the respect of your opponents and they are far less likely to attempt to deceive you. Be strong and innovative. Image is everything at the poker table. Never show weakness or frustration. Show conviction not vulnerability.

MACHIAVELLI SAID:

We have seen how necessary it is for a Prince to have his foundations well laid, otherwise it follows of necessity he will go to ruin. The chief foundations of all states, new as well as old or composite, are good laws and good arms.

Always play with plenty of chips in relation to the limits and be proactive in dictating the terms of play. These are the foundations that must be laid in order to achieve success at the poker table.

MACHIAVELLI SAID:

A Prince ought to have no other aim or thought, nor select anything else for his study, than war and its rules and discipline; for this is the sole art that belongs to him who rules, and it is of such force that it not only upholds those who are born princes, but it often enables men to rise from a private station to that rank. And, on the contrary, it is seen that when Princes have thought more of ease than arms, they have lost their states. And the first cause of your losing it is to neglect this art; what enables you to acquire a state is to be master of the art.

In today's society, the overwhelming majority of players are civilians. We honor civilian customs and laws, and we live by the etiquette of civilian society. When we enter the poker room, however, we must abandon this persona. We must adopt the mind-set of a general with the heart of a warrior. We must view our opponents as the enemy. If you are having a difficult time getting into the proper frame of mind, remember that your opponents are there to steal your money by any means necessary. Play with a heightened sense of awareness. Soldiers are trained to be prepared to attack at any time. Civilians are trained to be courteous and respectful of others. Since you do not know when opportunities will present themselves, you must be on guard at all times.

MACHIAVELLI SAID:

He ought never, therefore, to have out of his thoughts this subject of war, and in peace he should addict himself more to its exercise than in war; this he can do in two ways, the one by action, the other by study.

Since most of us spend the great majority of our lives outside of the poker room, it is difficult to make the transition to an entirely different mindset. Take time away from the poker room to study both poker and war theory. When you are sitting out hands, stay engaged. Study your opponents. Play the hand in your mind. Try to determine what your opponents have and how you would have played the hand. Most importantly, never let your guard down. There will be times when things seem too easy. Opponents will lay down for you. You will catch cards when you need to. No one will challenge you. In these circumstances, it is very easy to shed your Machiavellian self and go back to your civilian self. Do that and that nice stack of chips you just accumulated will disappear quickly.

MACHIAVELLI SAID:

As regards action, he ought above all things to . . . follow the chase incessantly, by which he accustoms his body to hardships, learns something of the nature of the localities, gets to find out how the mountains rise, how the valleys open out, and how the plains lie, to understand the nature of rivers and marshes, and, in all this, to take the greatest care.

Experience is critical in poker. Poker is a never-ending quest to succeed. Each hand begins anew and each hand is unique. However, with experience, you will learn how to handle adversity and how to avoid playing yourself into trouble spots. For example, many beginning players in hold'em cannot resist the urge to play any ace. This can be disastrous for such a player. If you are playing A, 9 and the flop brings an ace, what do you do? If another player stays, there is a great likelihood that he has a higher ace than you do. However, once in, many players find it hard to fold a pair of aces and end up losing more money on a hand that they never should have played in the first place. Play often and study situations. Learn what works for you and what does not. Get a feel for the types of hands you can play well. Learn to adapt to the situation. For instance, how you play a hand like pocket aces can vary greatly depending on the situation. If you have them in late position in a no limit ring game and you have three limpers and one raiser in front of you, you want to make a huge raise to get everyone out (or at least get heads-up) prior to the flop. On the other hand, say you are playing a no limit hold'em tournament in which you are just starting out with very small blinds and you find yourself with aces under the gun. A big bet here would not accomplish anything except winning the blinds. You may want to limp here or make a small raise in hopes someone acting behind you raises. Certainly, if someone raises behind you, you may then want to make a big re-raise. Poker is about playing every situation to maximum profits while minimizing your risk.

MACHIAVELLI SAID:
This knowledge is useful [to a Prince] in two ways: First, he learns to know his country and is better able to undertake its defense; second, afterwards, by means of the knowledge and observation of that locality, he understands with ease any other country that may be necessary for him to study thereafter because... with a knowledge of the aspects of one country, one can easily arrive at a knowledge of others.

Knowing how to avoid trouble spots is the first step in protecting your chips. While poker is a game of infinite possibilities, one can find many similarities in most hands and most players. With experience, a player can develop a keen awareness of when to avoid trouble and when to attack. With even more experience, good players will develop a sixth sense of when to implement deception and to recognize deceptive play in others. You must be knowledgeable in order to recognize moves from a knowledgeable opponent.

> **MACHIAVELLI SAID:**
> A wise Prince ought to...never in peaceful times stand idle, but he should increase his resources with industry in such a way that they may be available to him in adversity, so if Fortune chances, it may find him prepared to resist her blows.

Never get complacent at the poker table. Always seek ways to increase your bankroll. Be industrious and opportunistic. Play the entire situation, not just your cards. If you have a chance to steal the blinds in hold'em, then do so. If you sense weakness on your opponent's part, then exploit him. If your opponent makes a mistake, punish him. You will suffer your fair share of adversity and bad beats at the poker table. In order to survive and make a profit, you must not only take advantage of good fortune, but you must find ways to win money. As you gain experience, you will learn when to accumulate chips with minimum risk. In order to take advantage of any opportunity, however, it is critical that you are prepared to act at all times. You must be proactive in taking what you want. Treat each hand and turn to act with the careful and deliberate attention they deserve. There will be many hands when neither you nor your opponents have strong hands. In these situations, the first person to act usually wins the pot. Be the one to take uncontested pots.

> **MACHIAVELLI SAID:**
> [I]t is necessary for him to be sufficiently prudent so that he may know how to avoid the reproach of those vices that would lose him his state.

For successful players, poker is not a vice. They play because their superior skill and ability will allow them to win money consistently over the long term. Even if you are a recreational player, do not treat poker as a vice. Treat it as a competition that you want to excel in. Play smart and disciplined. Once you treat it as a vice, you are destined to lose. If your attitude is that I am here to play, not watch, then you become the weakest player at the table. At that point, your chips become meaningless and you will chase way too many hands.

If you sit down to the table with $100 with the mind-set that you have $100 to lose so long as you have a good time, then you are sure to lose that $100. By all means only play with an amount of money that you can afford to lose. But once you sit down, play to win. Do not squander chips needlessly. You can still be a recreational player. However, you will find that your enjoyment level will increase tremendously when you are playing to win and not just for entertainment value.

> **MACHIAVELLI SAID:**
> [E]very Prince ought to desire to be considered clement and not cruel.

Be a benevolent dictator at the poker table. Implement and enforce your rules to gain leadership, but let the other players believe you are friendly. Exploit your opponents' weaknesses, and punish their mistakes while maintaining an air of civility. Be subtle. Never let your opponents know how much you are dictating play.

> **MACHIAVELLI SAID:**
> [A Prince] ought to be slow to believe and to act, and he should not show fear, but proceed in a temperate manner with prudence and humanity so that too much confidence may not make him incautious and too much distrust render him intolerable.

Play with discipline at all times. Take calculated risks and mix up your play with unorthodox moves but let the game come to you. Do not force the action if you do not perceive an advantage. Be patient and wait for opportunities to exploit. They will come, even though you go through a spell where you do not see any.

Do not play scared. If you are playing not to lose, you cannot win. Keep the whims of Fortune in perspective. If the cards are coming your way, do not allow yourself to get overconfident. Conversely, if you suffer a bad beat, do not go on tilt. If you keep losing to the same opponent, do not lose your cool. No matter what the situation, keep your emotions in check. Remember, you are judged by the result over the long term. Always maintain an appearance of confidence in order to gain the respect of your opponents. Poker players can sense weakness from across the casino (and even over the Internet).

MACHIAVELLI SAID:
It is much safer to be feared than loved.

Play consistent, smart, and disciplined. Enforce your rules and dictate the play of the table. Be proactive and take what you want. Stay atop of the situation in order to adjust to the ever-changing circumstances. Adopt a soldier's mentality so that you are prepared to act at any time. Exploit your opponents' weaknesses and punish their mistakes. If you do these things, you will be feared at the poker table. While you do not want to incur the wrath of your opponents, you do not need their love either. If you have the respect of your opponents and they fear your play, you will be successful.

MACHIAVELLI SAID:
[F]ear preserves you by a dread of punishment, which never fails.

Punish your opponents' mistakes. Make them pay. Poker players do not like to lose money. If you consistently make them pay, they will fear you. A scared poker player is a losing poker player.

MACHIAVELLI SAID:
Nevertheless, a Prince ought to inspire fear in such a way that... he avoids hatred.

Do not inspire your opponents to take up arms against you. Let them use force with each other. If they fear you, but do not hate you, they will bend to your will.

MACHIAVELLI SAID:
A wise Prince should establish himself on that which is in his own control and not in that of others.

Play your game. If an opponent beats you by hitting his miracle card on the river when he had no business even playing the hand, do not get flustered. You can only control that which is within your power. You cannot control Fortune.

Poker is a game of imperfect information. There will be times when you guess wrong or you are caught bluffing. All you can do is keep on doing the things that will make you successful. Guessing wrong or getting caught bluffing can help you in the long term. You may gain valuable information about an opponent even when guessing wrong. When you are caught bluffing, you put your opponents on notice that you are not afraid to bluff. Next time when you catch a hand, you may be more likely to get paid off.

In addition, there will be plenty of hands where you do everything right but win. I have an extreme example of this from a recent no limit hold'em Internet tournament that I played. The buy-in was only $10, so I expected some very loose play. Well, the very first hand, I receive pocket aces under the gun. Since the blinds were very small relative to the starting chip stacks, I decide to make a small raise in hopes that someone behind me would make a big re-raise in an attempt to steal. Sure enough, the player to my immediate left makes a huge re-raise. Everyone folds to me. I go all-in, figuring there is enough money in the pot now to make it worth winning. Even if he calls, I will be an overwhelming favorite to win even more money. My opponent calls, and our cards are automatically turned over. He has K, 8 off suit. I do a double take to make sure I am reading his cards right. Yep, he has K, 8 off suit. (I knew players were loose in these low-limit-entry-fee tournaments, but this guy has exceeded my lowest of expectations.) Needless to say, I feel very good about my chances.

Then the flop brings an eight, and I just know I am going to lose. Sure enough, the turn brings another eight, the river is a blank, and I am the first one eliminated in the tournament—the first and only time that has ever happened to me. All I could do was laugh and turn off my computer.

While it is easy to laugh off a $10 entry fee (especially when it is impossible for me to second-guess my play), it reinforced an important lesson for me. Even if I am playing for much larger stakes, if I make a move that blows up on me, I have to shrug it off if it was the right move to make at the time.

MACHIAVELLI SAID:
Those Princes who have done great things have held good faith of little account and have known how to circumvent the intellect of men by craft.

The rules of polite society do not apply to the poker table. Deception is an integral part of the game. Those players who can implement it successfully will be winners. Deception is more than bluffing. It is about feigning strengths and hiding weaknesses. It is about getting your opponent to do something he should not do. It is about keeping your play unpredictable so that your opponent cannot figure out your play. If your opponent cannot figure out your play, he cannot effectively control his own play. Many solid players have a high intellect and can calculate pot odds quickly in just about every situation. While this is a solid foundation on which to build a game, the player who can read his opponent and adapt accordingly will have the upper hand every time over this player.

If you have difficulty implementing deceptive play, there are a few things you can do to make your play more unpredictable. For instance, you can pick a predetermined hand that you will play strong whenever you receive it. For instance, if you are about to play hold'em, pick a random playable hand like 8, 9 suited and tell yourself that every time you receive that hand, you are going to play it like K, K. By doing this, you accomplish a couple of things: First, you give yourself the chance to steal a pot with a drawing hand. Second, if you do hit a hand, no one will be able to put you on it. Finally, even if you get caught bluffing, you have put your opponents on notice that you are not afraid to mix it up. You can accomplish the same thing in seven card stud if every time you receive the ten of clubs as your first up card, you are going to play it with strength.

Another thing you can do is to occasionally pick a random hand before it is dealt and to tell yourself you are going to play it strong no matter what you are dealt. The theory is the same as the preceding, but here you are picking the moment rather than relying on receiving predetermined cards. Once you try these tricks a couple of times, you will get more comfortable executing bluffs, and soon you will be able to implement them on a strategic basis without the help of these aids.

Remember, there are no moral qualms in the poker room. Not only is deception tolerated, it is expected. Do not allow the fear of getting caught to keep you from bluffing. Many beginning players are embarrassed to get caught bluffing. Do not be. Anyone who implements deception will get caught at times. It is part of the game.

MACHIAVELLI SAID:

You must know there are two ways of contesting: the one by the law, the other by force; the first method is proper to men, the second to beasts. But because the first is frequently not sufficient, it is necessary to have recourse to the second. Therefore, it is essential for a Prince to understand how to avail himself of the man and the beast.

A solid fundamental grasp of poker strategy is essential to winning. You should know what hands are playable in every situation and how to play those hands in every situation. This is playing by the book. These rules may be sufficient against a table of novices; however, since most players will also have a solid grasp of the fundamentals, you will need to do more in order to be successful. Tap into your most primal self. Be hungry. Play with animal instincts.

You will have to use force. Your chips are your force. Know how to maximize that force. It is far better to play one hand with strength than two with weakness. Rather than make two $10 calls, make one raise. An amateur will make a play for the pot on fourth street, and if called, he will check the next time. An experienced player will make another play for the pot on fifth street. An effective use of your chips is critical to a winning poker strategy. Do not squander your chips. Learn to use them judiciously and with force, and you will be successful. Be reasoned and disciplined like a man. Have the killer instinct of a beast.

MACHIAVELLI SAID:

A Prince, therefore, being compelled knowingly to adopt the beast, ought to choose the fox and the lion because the lion cannot defend himself against snares and the fox cannot defend himself against wolves. Therefore, it is necessary to be a fox to discover the snares and a lion to terrify the wolves.

You must find the inner animal inside you for defense as well as offense. You must always be aware of those who will try to bully you and those who will try to deceive you. The nature of poker is such that good players can be bluffed out of pots when they are vulnerable. However, very good players are rarely trapped or baited into betting into a superior hand. A healthy amount of cynicism is good, but too much can be disastrous. Try to find the perfect balance between human reasoning and animal instincts. Play with hunger but not recklessness. Play with both drive and discipline. Have the cunning of the fox and the ferociousness of the lion.

MACHIAVELLI SAID:

And you have to understand this, that a Prince, especially a new one, cannot observe all those things for which men are esteemed, being often forced, in order to maintain the state, to act contrary to fidelity, friendship, humanity, and religion. Therefore, it is necessary for him to have a mind ready to turn itself accordingly, as the winds and variations of Fortune force it.

There are no moral dilemmas in the poker room. Poker players are esteemed for winning. Your sole object is to do everything within your power (outside of cheating, of course) to win. Lose your civilian self.

Adopt an internal code of conduct that affords you the flexibility to behave in ways that will maximize your profits.

You must have an objective view of both yourself and your opponents. You cannot have feelings of sympathy toward your opponent. While you must try to ascertain his mind-set, you do not want to empathize with your opponent. It is equally important to divorce certain feelings from yourself. If you win a big pot by drawing out, do not feel guilty about it. Conversely, if you are having a tough time of it, do not feel ashamed. So long as you are playing within your budget, do not feel bad about losing. Examine your play on an objective level. If you are making mistakes, correct them or take a break. If you are playing well but are suffering from the capriciousness of Fortune, stay the course. Do not be afraid to win. If you work hard at improving your game and do everything within your control to maximize your profits, then you deserve to win.

MACHIAVELLI SAID:
[I]n the actions of all men, and especially of Princes, who it is not prudent to challenge, one judges by the result.

In poker, you are judged by one thing and one thing only—how much money you win or lose. The result is very easy to determine. However, one should judge the results of a poker player over an extended period. In the short term, every poker player will suffer setbacks whether they are due to the whims of Fortune, bad play, or facing a superior opponent.

MACHIAVELLI SAID:
It makes him contemptible to be considered fickle, frivolous, effeminate, mean-spirited, and irresolute, all from which a Prince should guard himself *as from a rock*.

Self-analysis is critical in poker. While studying one's opponents is obviously important, you must not be so consumed with them that you neglect to analyze your own play. A comprehensive understanding of your opponents will not help you if you do not have a firm grasp of your own play. Always take the time to make sure that you are playing the way that you know you should be playing. If you are not employing the characteristics and attributes that you rely on for strong disciplined play, take a break. Come back after you have a chance to gather your thoughts. Do not come back until you have regained the confidence to play, as you know you should.

Above all else, you must consistently play objectively and with discipline. Do not tolerate self-defeating feelings. Do not play any differently against an obnoxious opponent as you would a kind opponent. In both cases, you should objectively get a read on their play. Do not allow any emotions you may feel play a part in how you play against them. How you play against each of them may be very different, but it should be based on an objective analysis of their game and style, not your personal feelings.

Do not be fickle. Poker can be a streaky game. If you are not getting cards, avoid feeling that you are "due." This will only cause you to play hands that you should not be playing. Conversely, if you are on a winning streak, avoid feeling that you cannot possibly win another hand. Every hand is completely separate and distinct from every other hand, and each should be played independently. Your recent history is only relevant to the extent that it helps you read your opponent or allows you to mix up your play. It has no bearing on what cards are coming or who is likely to get cards.

Do not be frivolous with your chips. Let your chips work for you. Do not commit them to the pot unless you perceive an advantage or you are getting value for the bet.

MACHIAVELLI SAID:
[H]e should endeavor to show in his actions, greatness, courage, gravity, and fortitude.

Work on being a strong player and projecting a strong image. Image is everything in poker. If your opponents respect and fear you, you will have a tremendous advantage.

MACHIAVELLI SAID:
[I]n his private dealings with his subjects, let him show that his judgments are irrevocable.

Whenever you play in a pot, play with strength. Again, it is better to play one hand with strength than two with weakness. Whenever you are ahead in a hand, your opponents should know that it will be expensive and that they will not be receiving free cards. Whenever you are in a pot, your opponents should know that they will have a tough time outplaying you unless they have the cards.

Playing with strength accomplishes two goals: First, it maximizes your profits in that you will win many pots when your opponent is weak regardless of what cards you are holding. Next, it will minimize your losses, for you will know an opponent is strong when he fights back against you.

MACHIAVELLI SAID:
[A]nd maintain himself in such a reputation that no one can hope either to deceive him or to get around him.

Be cognizant of the reputation that you are projecting. If you are playing hold'em, do not always fold in the small blind when you do not have a strong hand. In stud, do not always lay down a hand on the river when you miss a draw. Choose times to fight back. Let your opponents know that it will be difficult to deceive you or chase you out. To do otherwise leaves you vulnerable. If opponents know you will lay down a hand whenever you miss your draw, they will always bet into you even if they have missed as well.

MACHIAVELLI SAID:
That Prince is highly esteemed who conveys this impression of himself, and he who is highly esteemed is not easily conspired against; for, provided it is well known that he is an excellent man and revered by his people, he can only be attacked with difficulty.

The right image in poker is critical to success. If you follow Machiavelli's advice for being a strong and powerful leader, you will project the right image. It will take hard work, and images must be earned. However, once you have earned a reputation as a strong player who can dictate the terms of play, the table will open up to you. Other players will avoid you. Opponents will alter their play around yours. Players will not challenge you. When a player does challenge you, you can be sure he has a strong hand. Their play will be predictable. In addition, you will have more opportunities. Players will fold marginal hands when they know you have yet to act behind them. It takes hard work and discipline to play the Machiavellian way, but the rewards are well worth it.

MACHIAVELLI SAID:
Never ... imagine that [you] can choose perfectly safe courses; rather, expect to have to take very doubtful ones, because it is found in ordinary affairs that one never seeks to avoid one trouble without running into another.

In poker, trouble is always just around the corner. Unless you have the nuts, never give your opponents free cards. Do not try to outlast your opponents or back into winning hands. If you are in the lead, bet big. In the end, this is much more cost-effective than making a small bet or call because you do not want to risk too much on one hand. Poker cannot be played risk free. You can, however, minimize that risk by playing with strength and discipline. I cannot count the number of times I have heard a player announce that he has aces on fourth street in seven card stud.

The following is a typical situation I have witnessed countless times in a $1–$5 stud game. About five players stay for a $1 bet after the first three cards are dealt. On fourth street, a player with a J up card receives an ace. He bets $5 and, to his surprise and dismay, gets four callers. At this point, he says aloud, "Geez, nobody here is afraid of aces." Many players mistakenly think this is a bluff. However, in just about every case, the player really does have aces. So why does he tell his opponents? Because he wants them to fold, and he is frustrated that he has been unable to accomplish this with a big bet. While he is confident that he has the best hand right now, he does not want four other players attempting to draw out on him. He wants to win the pot or, at the very least, get heads-up with one opponent. While his chances of winning against one opponent are very good, he is an underdog against four opponents collectively.

The point of this story is not to suggest that you announce your hand to your opponents. In fact, that is against the rules of most casinos, and your hand could be ruled dead. The point of the story is to illustrate how important it is to play with strength and discipline. Typically, the player with aces who gets four callers is a player who does not have the respect and fear of his opponents. When you do not have the respect and fear of your opponents, you leave yourself vulnerable even when you have good hands.

MACHIAVELLI SAID:
A Prince ought also to show himself a patron of ability and to honor the proficient in every art.

Be a well-rounded poker player. Become proficient at a number of games. Work on every aspect of your play. The art of poker is a never-ending learning process. Always strive to improve your game. Take the time to reflect on your play so that you can recognize and work on your weaknesses. As poker increases in popularity, you will see many more highly skilled players. The slightest edge will make the difference between winning and losing. Your margin of error will be minimal. To succeed, you must work on every aspect of your game.

MACHIAVELLI SAID:
[T]hat deliverance is of no avail, when you do not depend on yourself; those are only reliable, certain, and durable who depend on themselves and their valour.

The only thing you can rely on at the poker table is your ability. There will be times when you will get bailed out by Fortune, but do not allow that to cloud your judgment. If you are relying on luck, go play slots. Recently, I played a limit hold'em tournament, and we were down to the final three tables after starting with 160 players. The final two tables would finish *in the money*. The blinds were $500–$1,000 and the average chip stack was about $10,000. I was in the small blind and looked at my cards to see 9, 4 off-suit. There were a couple of callers in early position, and on a hunch, I made up my mind that I would call. I had an average stack, and since I was playing to win and not just finish in the money, I thought it would be a good opportunity to make a play for the pot if the flop either helped me or appeared not to help anyone else. Most importantly, though, was this overwhelming hunch that I had.

Well, before the action got to me, the player to my immediate right raised. At this point, I had no choice but to fold. The flop came 9, 4, 4. Two other players had 9's, and they proceeded to raise each other back and forth. If I had stayed, I would have won an enormous pot. I was completely upset with myself for not playing this hand. A few hands later, I raised pre-flop under the gun with A, 5 suited on another hunch (I thought I was on to something since my previous hunch would have paid off), and I took a beating. Soon thereafter, I was eliminated. Afterward, I examined my play and realized I had made two big mistakes: First, when I was sitting with 9, 4 off suit in the small blind, I should not have looked at my cards until it was my turn to act. If I had waited, then in the face of a raise, I never would have had my hunch and I never would have second-guessed myself for folding. The next, and bigger, mistake was believing that I now somehow possessed a sixth sense that was worth acting on. By acting on a hunch, I was hoping to get lucky rather than relying on my skill to advance.

MACHIAVELLI SAID:
I hold it to be true that Fortune is the arbiter of one half of our actions, but she still leaves us to direct the other half.

At the time of its publication, Machiavelli's preceding statement was revolutionary in that he believed man could, to some extent, control his destiny. Taken in today's context, that same statement may appear fatalistic.

However as anyone who has ever played poker can attest, the concept that Fortune is responsible for one half of our actions is dead-on accurate as it applies to the poker table. The confidence and the ability to control that other half is what separates winning poker players from losing ones. The recognition and acceptance that Fortune will play a large role at the poker table is what separates winning poker players from losing ones. Having the foresight to prepare for the whims of Fortune is what separates winning poker players from losing ones. Finally, how one reacts when Fortune delivers a serious blow is what separates winning poker players from losing ones.

MACHIAVELLI SAID:
I compare [Fortune] to one of those raging rivers, which when in flood overthrows the plains, sweeping away trees and buildings and bearing away the soil from place to place; everything flies before it, all yield to its violence, without being able in any way to withstand it, and yet, though its nature be such, it does not follow therefore that men, when the weather becomes fair, shall not make provision, both with defenses and barriers, in such a manner that, rising again, the waters may pass away by canal and their force be neither so unrestrained nor so dangerous. So it happens with Fortune, who shows her power where valor has not prepared to resist her, and thither she turns her forces where she knows that barriers and defenses have not been raised to constrain her.

As anyone who has suffered a bad beat on the river can attest, Fortune can cut an ugly swath at the poker table while putting a significant dent in your wallet. Thus, you must do everything in your power to defend against Fortune. Fortune is as big an enemy as any opponent at the table. Do not give her a chance to beat you. Do not give free cards. Do not allow opponents to chase runners. Do not chase runners yourself. Play with a purpose and with an advantage. Do not play hoping to get lucky. If you are feeling lucky, go play roulette.

When you do suffer bad luck, remember that it is part of poker. Do not get frustrated. Do not try to get even. Do not mistakenly believe that

Fortune now owes you. Just keep playing your game. If you stay on your game and play effectively, you will build a reserve that will protect you from your share of bad luck.

MACHIAVELLI SAID:

The Prince who relies entirely on Fortune is lost when it changes.

Recognize who is winning because of Fortune and who is winning due to skill. Make sure to include yourself in the analysis. Whoever is winning because of luck will eventually lose.

MACHIAVELLI SAID:

He will be successful who directs his actions according to the spirit of the times, and he whose actions do not accord with the times will not be successful.

The situation at a poker table can change rapidly. Players come and go, players change seats, chips change hands, and Fortune changes direction. Those players who can adjust the quickest to the ever-changing circumstances will be successful. Stay focused at all times so that you not only can stay aware of the situation but also can anticipate how the situation will be changing in the near future. Make sure you consider all the factors comprising the situation at the table. Look at your own chip stack and play, but do not be so focused on yourself that you fail to recognize all the other changes taking place at the table.

MACHIAVELLI SAID:

Because men are involved in affairs that lead to the end that every man has before him, namely, glory and riches, they still get there by various methods: one with caution, and another with haste; one by force, another by skill; one by patience, and another by its opposite. Each one succeeds in reaching the goal by a different method.

Play with a style that suits your game. Do not force yourself to be something that you are not. There are very successful poker players of all types. Some find success by being super aggressive. Others win with a patient, conservative style. Play in a way that you feel comfortable and that will maximize your profits.

> **MACHIAVELLI SAID:**
> One can also see two cautious men: one attaining his end, the other failing; similarly, two men by different observances are equally successful, the one being cautious, the other impetuous. All this arises from nothing else than whether they conform in their methods to the spirit of the times.

No matter what your style, however, you will have to adapt to the situation. For example, say you are playing a no limit tournament and you are generally a tight aggressive player who waits for strong hands or opportunities to play with strength. You find yourself on the verge of being short-stacked but still with enough chips to play with some force. However, when the blinds increase after the next few hands, you may not have enough force to scare anyone away. At this point, you do not have the luxury of waiting for a strong hand to play. You must get aggressive if you are going to survive in the tournament.

Conversely, take the aggressive player who likes to bet early and often in order to bully his opponents and establish his dominance. This strategy will not work against a number of loose opponents who will call down any bet no matter what they are holding. Against these types of opponents, you want to wait for a winning hand for you are sure to be paid off.

Never stay wedded to the same strategy. Stay abreast of the situation so that you can adapt your play, and you will be successful. In addition, take note of how well your opponents adapt to the situation. What previously worked against an opponent in the past may not work in the future if they adjust properly.

MACHIAVELLI SAID:
Changes in estate also issue from this, for if one governs himself with caution and patience, times and affairs will converge in such a way so that his administration is successful and his fortune is made; but if times and affairs change, he is ruined if he does not change his course of action. But a man is not often found sufficiently circumspect to know how to accommodate himself to the change, both because he cannot deviate from what nature inclines him to do and because, having always prospered by acting in one way, he cannot be persuaded that it is well to leave it. Therefore, the cautious man, when it is time to turn adventurous, does not know how to do it; hence, he is ruined. But had he changed his conduct with the times, Fortune would not have changed.

It is extremely difficult to change one's style and strategy especially when one is riding a wave of success. For example, observe the super aggressive player in a no limit tournament. He has managed to build a big chip lead as the tournament has dwindled to fourteen players. Only the final nine players will be in the money. This player may decide to tighten up now. By playing conservatively, he knows he can reach the final table with a sizable chip stack. If, on the other hand, this player is unable to adjust, he runs the risk of not even making the final table with his super aggressive play.

While you must stay extremely focused when playing in order to stay atop of the situation, it is also important to pull away from the game at times in order to remain objective. Remember to periodically detach yourself from the game in order to analyze your play and style and to decide how you can adjust to the ever-changing circumstances. Our own play is the only thing we can ultimately control at the poker table, which is why it is critical to take the time to ensure that we are doing everything within our power to take advantage of the current situation.

Machiavelli's *The Seven Books on the Art of War* contain numerous insights that are as relevant today as they were when they were first written.

Certain passages have an uncanny application to the modern-day poker room. These maxims are analyzed below:

MACHIAVELLI SAID:
[T]here is nothing that has less in common with another, and that is so dissimilar, as civilian life is from the military. Thus, it is often observed, if anyone designs to avail himself of an enlistment in the army, that he soon changes not only his clothes but also his customs, his habits, his voice.... For I do not believe that any man can dress in civilian clothes who wants to be quick and ready for any violence, nor can that man have civilian customs and habits, who judges those customs to be effeminate and those habits not conducive to his actions, nor does it seem right to him to maintain his ordinary appearance and voice who, with his beard and cursing, wants to make other men afraid.

While the poker room is certainly not comparable to war, the mind-set and mentality needed to succeed in the poker room is at odds with our everyday personas. The minute you sit down at the table, you must shed your everyday self. Sure, you can be civil and courteous, but you are not there to make peace. You are not there to compromise. You are not there to find common ground. You are there to win. You are there to defend your chips from everyone else at the table while simultaneously attempting to siphon chips away from your competitors. If you were lined up against an opposing lineman in football, you would attack because you know you would get hurt if you did not. Do not be misled by the cordial atmosphere that surrounds most felt tables. Everyone is there to compete. Anyone who fails to do so will get hurt—financially.

MACHIAVELLI SAID:
[I]t is necessary to examine what arms the ancients used, and from them, select the best.

Poker is a never-ending learning process. Not only should you learn from your own play, but you should analyze the play of others. Study the play of players whom you respect. Read as much as you can. Discuss strategy with other players. Share hand histories with confidants and ask them how they would have played. Poker is a game of imperfect information. Whatever you can do to increase your poker IQ will provide you with a significant edge.

MACHIAVELLI SAID:
[T]he Romans used the sword for offense, and for defense, the shield.

In poker, a good defense is as critical as a good offense. Work and develop the weapons and skills necessary for both. Poker requires a never-ending balance between chip preservation and chip accumulation.

MACHIAVELLI SAID:
[T]he Romans were superior in virtù, kinds of arms, and discipline.

The elements of virtù, a large chip stack, and discipline are the skills necessary to succeed in poker. Without virtù, you cannot accumulate a large chip stack. Without discipline, you cannot maintain a large chip stack.

MACHIAVELLI SAID:
Thus, whoever considers the advantages and disadvantages of one and the other will see that the one without armor has no remedy, but the one well armored will have no difficulty in overcoming the first blow and the first passes of the pike.

Whoever plays poker will suffer periods of misfortune, lousy cards, and bad beats. Those players who possess virtu, a sizable chip stack, and discipline will survive these periods without breaking down or going on tilt.

A successful poker player is a complete player equipped to handle every situation.

MACHIAVELLI SAID:
[A]lthough the Romans prized their own discipline and trusted their arms (and armor), if they had to select a place, either one where it was rough enough to protect themselves from the horses and where they could not deploy their forces or one where they had more to fear from the horses but where they were able to spread out, they would always take the latter and leave the former.

As important as defense is, do not become so consumed with it that you take yourself out of the game. You must always be in position to attack when the opportunity presents itself. If you play not to lose, you cannot win.

MACHIAVELLI SAID:
[The Romans] trained their youth to make them speedy in running, dexterous in jumping, and strong in driving stakes and wrestling. And these three qualities are almost always necessary in a soldier; for speed makes him adept at occupying places before the enemy arrives, to come upon him unexpectedly and to pursue him when he is routed. Dexterity makes him adept at avoiding blows. Strength makes him better at carrying arms, hurling himself against an enemy, and sustaining an attack.

Speed, dexterity, and strength are essential skills for a poker player. Speed allows you to act quickly when you sense your opponent is vulnerable. Be the first to make a play at the pot, and you will put your opponent on the defensive. Implement check-raises to catch your opponent off guard. Never let up when you have the better of an opponent. Be prepared at all times so that you are ready to act and can avoid giving away tells.

Dexterity is the ability to recognize when you should get out of a pot. It is never too late to get out of a pot if you do not have the best of it. Sure, there are times when you are getting overwhelming pot odds to stay, and you should stay. But do not compound a mistake by believing you are committed to a pot. You always have options. Exercise them. If you are playing seven card hi-lo and you start with J♥, J♣, 10♣, fold to a raise from any up card higher than a Jack. You do not have to play hands that can get you in trouble.

Because there is a lot of luck in poker, strength takes on added importance. When you have the lead in a hand, put your chips to work for you. Your chips are your arms. Use them as force to keep opponents from drawing out on you. Implementing your chips with strength is the most effective way to deal with Fortune. When you do suffer a bad beat, have the strength to fight it off and remain disciplined. Keep playing within your game.

MACHIAVELLI SAID:
The Romans wanted their soldiers to wound the enemy by stabbing him, rather than by slashing, because such a blow was more fatal and the enemy had less defense against it, and because it left the wounded unprotected, permitting a soldier to be more adept at repeating his attack than he would be by slashing.

The biggest mistake players can make in no limit poker is to bet an insufficient amount when they are trying to protect their hand and keep an opponent from drawing out on them. Players feel more vulnerable when they bet a greater amount when, in fact, the opposite is true. A weak bet is much more likely to be called or raised. The stronger the bet you make, the greater the likelihood that you win the pot. Thus, you are better protected and less vulnerable by making a bigger bet, even though you are putting more money at risk.

MACHIAVELLI SAID:
[I]t is not the splendor of jewels and gold that makes the enemy submit themselves to you, but only the fear of arms.

When choosing a game, always pick a limit that will allow you to sit down with a large chip stack compared with the rest of the table. Your chips are your arms. Implement them judiciously and with strength, and your opponents will fear you.

MACHIAVELLI SAID:
[K]nowing how to fight makes men more audacious, as no one fears to do the things that he has been taught to do.

There is no substitute for experience. Poker is a game of infinite possibilities. It is also a game that requires great confidence in order to be successful. Take full advantage of every poker experience to learn as much as you can. Pay close attention to every hand whether or not you are involved in the pot. Increase your poker IQ so that you will be able to play with confidence—even when you face a new situation.

MACHIAVELLI SAID:
[I]t is not enough in undertaking good training to have hardened men made strong, fast, and dexterous, but it is necessary to teach them to be disciplined...[a]nd without a doubt, bold but undisciplined men are weaker than the timid but disciplined ones for discipline drives away fear from men; lack of discipline makes the bold act foolishly.

Poker is a long and tedious exercise. As such, it requires a great deal of discipline to succeed over the long run. It takes discipline to avoid playing Q, 7 off-suit in hold'em when you have not played a hand in over an hour. It takes discipline to avoid going on tilt when you suffer a bad beat. It takes discipline to mix up your play in order to make it appear unpredictable when in fact you are playing with a purpose. It takes discipline to avoid overconfidence when the cards are falling your way. Do not confuse discipline with timidity. Successful players do not needlessly play many hands. When they do play, they play with strength. When you play a lot of hands, you lose a lot of hands, and you will soon find yourself playing with scared money. When you play judiciously, you will find yourself playing without fear of losing.

MACHIAVELLI SAID:
[A]mong every ten men there is one of more life, of more heart, or, at least, of more authority, who with his courage, with words, and by example keeps the others firm.

Hold'em and Omaha tables typically have up to ten seats while stud games typically seat eight. Each game contains a small enough group to allow one individual who embodies all the .qualities of virtu to take charge. Be that person.

MACHIAVELLI SAID:
The greatest mistake that men make who arrange an army for an encampment is to give it only one front and commit it to only one onrush and one attempt.

If a pot is worth making a play for, do not give up after one attempt. If you semi-bluff after the flop and are called, be prepared to bet again after the turn if you believe your opponent is vulnerable. Stick with a position. Not only will this increase your chances of winning the pot, but it will help your overall game and table image. If after you are called, you consistently check, your opponents will pick up on this and will be more likely to stay in a pot with you if they know they can get free cards by calling once. A sure sign of an amateur is a player who only makes one attempt at a pot.

MACHIAVELLI SAID:
It is more important to guard against being shot than shooting the enemy.

Poker requires a constant and delicate balance between protecting your own chip stack and acquiring your opponents' chips. While you do not want to play so conservatively that you do not give yourself the opportunity to acquire chips, keep in mind that it is imperative to avoid losing your stake. Without an adequate chip stack, you cannot compete.

MACHIAVELLI SAID:
[I]f the enemy abandons it, you seize it.

If your opponent does not want the pot, make sure you take it.

MACHIAVELLI SAID:
[I]f you do not want something fired from a distance to injure you, there is no other remedy than to seize it as quickly as possible.

Do not let opponents draw out on you. If you are ahead, seize the pot. If you are playing no limit, bet enough to keep opponents from coming from a great distance behind to beat you.

MACHIAVELLI SAID:
There is nothing that causes greater confusion in an army than to obstruct its vision, from which most stalwart armies have been routed for having their vision obstructed either by dust or by the sun.

Incorporate some deception into your game. Implement a level of deception in which you are comfortable and in which you are able to keep playing with discipline. Do not worry about getting caught. If you do, it still serves its purpose in that it will help keep your opponents guessing.

MACHIAVELLI SAID:
[A] good captain and a good army do not have to fear an injury that is confined, but a general one. They also imitate the Swiss who never shun an engagement even if terrified by artillery, but rather they punish with death those who because they fear the engagement either break ranks or give the sign of fear by their actions.

Do not play with fear. Scared money is dead money. If you play not to lose, you cannot win. This does not, however, mean that you should be a calling station. Always play smart and with discipline. Within the course of your game, be aggressive and challenge opponents. When you sense fear in your opponent, do not let up on him. Keep punishing him until he fights back.

MACHIAVELLI SAID:

There is not greater peril than to overextend the front of your army, unless you have a very large and very brave army; otherwise you have to make it rather wide and of short depth than of long length and very narrow. For when you have a small force compared to the enemy, you ought to seek other remedies.

Your chips are your force. Do not sit down at a table if you are going to be short-stacked. Rather, go play a lower limit game. Use your chips wisely. Engage them to maximize their force. It is far better to play one hand aggressively than two hands passively. If you are playing a high ante or blind game, avoid limping in. Rather, wait for opportune times to raise. Do not spread your chips too thin. Bundle them to increase their force. You will find it more profitable to raise once rather than to call twice.

MACHIAVELLI SAID:

If the enemy is of a lesser number, you ought to seek wide places.

When you have a substantial chip advantage over an opponent, exploit that advantage. Challenge him if he is playing with fear. Bet out with semi-bluffing hands. Do everything you can to put him on the defensive. If he is playing scared, then play more hands than you normally would in order to take advantage of his weak play.

MACHIAVELLI SAID:

[I]n rough and difficult places, you do not have the advantage of being able to avail yourself of (all) your ranks.

Avoid playing hands that can get you into trouble. A hand like A, 9 in hold'em should be avoided. If you flop an ace, there is a good chance you are up against a higher ace. Then what do you do? You do not want to fold, but you cannot risk raising into a stronger hand, so you call the hand down and lose three more bets on a hand you never should have played in the first place.

MACHIAVELLI SAID:

[P]art of your forces can be well hidden so that the enemy may be assaulted suddenly and without his expecting it, which will always be the cause of giving you victory.

Winning poker is more than winning hands. It is maximizing profits. To maximize your profits, your play must be unpredictable. If your opponent can put you on a hand, you will never get paid off. If you only play the nuts, everyone will fold when you finally have the nuts. Do not be afraid to bluff. The bluff may win you the hand right there. Even if you are called, however, you have shown your capability to bluff and have increased your chances of getting paid off the next time you do have a strong hand. Do not overplay a strong hand—especially against an aggressive opponent. Let him do the betting for you, and then raise on the later, more expensive streets.

MACHIAVELLI SAID:

The enemy cavalry may be easily disturbed by unusual forms.

Implement deception. Try some unorthodox moves. Do things to keep your opponents off their game. If your opponent cannot get a read on your play, then he cannot fully control his own play. When your opponent cannot fully control his own play, you gain an advantage.

MACHIAVELLI SAID:

When one wins, he ought to follow up the victory with all speed.

Poker is a game of streaks. It is also a very emotional game. If you are enjoying success, allow yourself to play more aggressively. Do not get overconfident or reckless. Rather, stay disciplined and within your game, but
play more aggressively to take advantage of your opponents' emotional
state. Players tend to play very cautiously against an opponent on a hot
streak.

MACHIAVELLI SAID:
Caesar never rested after a victory, but pursued the routed enemy
with great impetus and fury until he had completely assaulted it.

Never rest on your laurels, and never have sympathy for an opponent.
Play every situation to maximum profits. No one will have sympathy for
you when your luck is running bad. The poker room is not the real world. You
should not have any moral qualms about your behavior. You are expected
to do everything within your control to maximize your profits.

MACHIAVELLI SAID:
But when one loses, a captain ought to see if something useful to
him can result from this loss, especially if some residue of his army
remains.

Win or lose, always take the time to evaluate your play. There will be times
when you do everything right but win. There will be other times when you
make critical mistakes or you could have done something differently. There
will even be other times when you read your opponent correctly: you know
he has you beat and you call him anyway. Evaluate every situation. Did
you play correctly? Did you misread your opponent? Did your opponent
outplay you? Did you have a mental breakdown or emotional lapse? Learn
from your mistakes.

MACHIAVELLI SAID:
An opportunity can arise from the unawareness of the enemy,

which frequently becomes obscured after a victory and gives you
the occasion to attack him.

Novices often get overconfident when they are winning, leaving them vulnerable. Look for opportunities to exploit players when they begin to play
with reckless abandon.

> **MACHIAVELLI SAID:**
> It is seen, therefore, that there is nothing so capable of success as
> that which the enemy believes you cannot attempt, because men
> are often injured more when they are less apprehensive. A captain
> ought, therefore, when he cannot do this, at least endeavor with
> industry to restrict the injury caused by the defeat. And to do this,
> it is necessary for you to take steps that the enemy is not able to
> follow easily or that give him cause for delay.

Lure your opponents into a false sense of confidence. Let them think you
will not challenge them and then pounce on them after they have done
your betting for you. Conversely, if you are on a draw, raise on the early
streets to slow down your opponent on the more expensive rounds in
order to get a free card. For example, if you are playing seven card stud
and you have four hearts on fourth street and you believe your opponent
has a high pair, then raise him. If you hit the flush on fifth street, you will
already have an extra bet in the pot. If you miss on fifth street (when the
betting limits go up), your opponent is likely to check to you, giving you
a free card and another shot at the flush.

> **MACHIAVELLI SAID:**
> Necessity arises when you see that by not fighting you must lose in
> an event; for example, when you see you are about to lack money,
> and therefore your army has to be dissolved in any case; when
> hunger is about to assail you; or when you expect the enemy to be
> reinforced again by new forces. In these cases, one ought always to
> fight, even with your disadvantage, for it is much better to try your

fortune when it can favor you than not to try and surely see your ruin. In such a case, it is as serious an error for a captain not to fight as it is to pass up an opportunity to win, either from ignorance or from cowardice.

When playing in tournaments, you must take a chance while you still have the force of your chips. To do otherwise is to guarantee defeat. If you allow the blinds or antes to eat away at your stack without making a move, you cannot win. It is much better to take a chance and give yourself the opportunity to win. You cannot wait for a premium hand to play. Play a good drawing hand in a multiway pot, so if you hit, you will win a big pot. Or bet aggressively with a marginal hand while you still have enough chips to force opponents to fold.

> **MACHIAVELLI SAID:**
> The enemy sometimes gives you the advantage, and sometimes (it derives from) your prudence.

Exploit your opponents' mistakes. Do not just play your cards blindly. Play the situation and look to take advantage of your opponents' play. Play your opponents and the situation as well as your cards.

> **MACHIAVELLI SAID:**
> If the enemy has diminished in strength, you ought to try your fortune.

Attack short stacks. Play more hands than you normally would against a weak opponent, for you will have plenty of chances to outplay him during the course of a hand.

> **MACHIAVELLI SAID:**
> Consider the location in which [you] are and if it is more suitable for the enemy than for [you], consider which of [you] has the better

convenience of supply, and consider whether it is better to delay
the engagement or undertake it.

Be cognizant of the entire situation. If you do not perceive an advantage, do
not play the hand. That advantage could be cards, position, or a tell from your
opponent. If your opponent has an advantage, fold. Why play into your opponent's hand? Wait until you have an advantage before you commit chips.

MACHIAVELLI SAID:
[I]f the enemy has a much larger force than you do and in order to
disorganize you wants to assault you on several sides, it will be his
foolishness and his gamble, for to do this, he must go (spread) himself thin so that you can always attack on one side and resist on
another, and in a brief time ruin him.

Do not back down from large stacks. If an opponent wants to try to bully
you, take advantage of it. Wait until you have an advantage and let him
bet into you. Challenge him when he is vulnerable and he thinks he can
chase you out of the pot. If he insists on throwing his chips around to try
to intimidate his opponents, his stack will diminish quickly.

MACHIAVELLI SAID:
[G]uard against ambushes, which may happen in two ways: either
you enter into them while marching or you are cunningly drawn
into them by the enemy without your being aware of it.

Always be on guard for another player trying to trap you. Remember that
your opponents are trying to maximize their profits the same as you.
Study your opponents so that you know how they will try to do this. Pay
attention even when you are not in the pot.

MACHIAVELLI SAID:
As to the second case, being drawn into them (which our men call

being drawn into a trap), you ought to be aware and not believe
readily in those things that appear to be less reasonable than they
should be, as would be the case if an enemy places some booty
before you, you might believe it to be (an act of) love, but it could
conceal deceit inside it.

If you know your opponent, you will know when he is doing something
out of the ordinary that should raise your suspicions.

MACHIAVELLI SAID:
[Y]ou should never believe that the enemy does not know his
business; rather, if you want to deceive yourself less and bring on
less danger, then the more he appears weak and the more enemy
appears more cautious is the time you ought to esteem (be
wary of) him.

Respect your opponents. You cannot defeat your opponent if you do not respect his capabilities. Understand your opponent's capabilities so that
you can understand his weaknesses. With this knowledge, you can avoid
playing into his strengths while exploiting his weaknesses.

MACHIAVELLI SAID:
[I]f you want the encampment to be safe, it must be *strong* and
organized.

To adopt a Machiavellian strategy is to play in a strong and disciplined
manner. Be organized in order to implement your chips efficiently. This
will allow you to maximize the effectiveness of your chips.

MACHIAVELLI SAID:
No captain encamps near the enemy, unless he is disposed to come
to an engagement whenever the enemy wants.

Whenever you put chips in the pot, you must be prepared for a battle. Every time you bet or raise (or call when there are still players to act behind you), you are subject to a raise. In addition, unless you are on the river, there are more betting rounds to follow. In the great majority of cases, you should not commit money to the pot when you are subject to a raise unless you are prepared to call that raise. Otherwise, you risk being sucked in and calling additional bets because you feel you already have some money invested in the pot. If you do not perceive an advantage or sense an opportunity to exploit, you should fold rather than play marginal hands that have the potential to suck you in and cost you a lot of money. When you enter a pot, you are entering the battlefield and are subject to attack from any other player who enters that battlefield.

MACHIAVELLI SAID:
Such diligence results in the enemy not being able to have correspondence with your military leaders and not to have co-knowledge of your counsels.

Never give away information when you do not have to.

MACHIAVELLI SAID:
The laws for their enforcement should be harsh and hard, and the executor very hard.

When your opponents make a mistake, punish them. The failure to do so will cost you money.

MACHIAVELLI SAID:
Because where there are severe punishments, there also ought to be rewards so that men should fear and hope at the same time.

Because there is a large element of luck in poker, even the worst players will win pots occasionally. That is the only thing that keeps them coming back for more. So encourage them. Even if they hit their one out on the river to beat you for a huge pot, congratulate them on their gutsy play.

MACHIAVELLI SAID:
It also helps one in freeing himself from the enemy to do something that keeps him at bay. This is done in two ways: either by assaulting him with part of your forces, so that while intent on the battle, he gives the rest of your forces the opportunity to save themselves or by having some new incident spring up, which, by the novelty of the thing, makes him wonder and, for this reason, become apprehensive and stand still.

If you are in a battle for a pot and you sense your opponent has not improved, then bet into or raise him. Try to win the pot right there so that you do not have to jeopardize more chips by calling your opponent down to the river. If you catch a scare card that does not improve your hand, then check-raise your opponent in order to give him something to think about and make him apprehensive.

MACHIAVELLI SAID:
A captain ought, among all the other actions of his, endeavor with every art to divide the forces of the enemy by giving him cause so that he has to separate his forces and, because of this, become weaker.

Every time you can cause an opponent to lose chips, you weaken him. If you are in a multiway pot with the nuts and the person in front of you bets, do not raise if that will cause the person behind you to fold. Keep everyone in, and maximize how many chips each commits. How you play your strong hands is critical to your overall success. The more chips you can win accomplishes two goals: First, it enriches you right away. Second, it weakens your opponent, which will prove profitable to you in later hands.

MACHIAVELLI SAID:
Sometimes it helps to deceive the enemy by changing one of your
habits, relying on which, he is ruined.

No matter how much you mix up your play, constantly reevaluate how
you are playing to ensure that you are not doing anything predictable.

MACHIAVELLI SAID:
There is nothing more imprudent or more perilous to a captain than
to wage war in winter.

History is full of examples of wars lost by stubborn leaders who chose to
do battle in conditions not best suited for their armies. Do not engage an
opponent in a battle over a pot if you do not have an advantage. That advantage can be having better cards, better position, or a perception that
your opponent is vulnerable. However, if you cannot sense an advantage,
do not enter the engagement. Why do battle with conditions that benefit
your opponent?

MACHIAVELLI SAID:
All the industry used in military discipline is used in order to be
organized to undertake an engagement with your enemy, as this is
the end toward which a captain must aim.

Remember that your goal is to defeat your opponents. All your energy
should be directed toward that goal. You cannot blindly play your cards.
Your goal is not to make good hands. Your goal is to defeat your opponent.
If you have a strong hand but your opponent has a stronger hand, then
fold. If your opponent is vulnerable, then you can defeat your opponent
regardless of what cards you hold.

MACHIAVELLI SAID:
Whoever, therefore, does not want the forces, organization, disci-

pline, and virtù, in some part, to be of value, makes war in the field
in the wintertime. And because the Romans wanted to avail themselves of all these things, into which they put so much industry,
they avoided not only the wintertime but also rough mountains and
difficult places and anything else that could impede their ability to
demonstrate their skill and virtù.

Give yourself the chance to win. Do not play when you do not have the
advantage. If you have skill, then allow that skill to win for you. Play when
you have the better of it and you can manipulate your opponents. Do not
play when you are vulnerable and cannot get a good read on your opponent. Do not limp in with marginal hands that can only get you in trouble. Do not think you can call cheaply when there are still players behind
you ready to act. If you possess discipline, virtu, and poker skill, then
enter pots when you can maximize those skills. Play hands when you can
be the leader, and control the pot. Do not play someone else's pot.

MACHIAVELLI SAID:
[N]o one ought to do anything that through the medium of which
you begin to lose your reputation without any remedy, the loss of
which makes others consider you less.

Everything you do at the poker table is being observed and analyzed by
your opponents. Every move you make not only will affect the current pot
but will have an effect on how others play against you in future pots.
Cultivate the proper image to become the leader of your table. Never let
your guard down and never get careless. As soon as you go on tilt, your
opponents will pounce on you instantly. Protect your reputation at all
costs.

MACHIAVELLI SAID:
[P]rovision yourself, and deprive the enemy of the opportunity to
avail himself of the resources of our country.

Protect your chip stack. Every time you lose a chip, not only do you weaken yourself, but you strengthen the enemy.

MACHIAVELLI SAID:
One ought to take care not to be able to be taken by hunger. [I]t has been said that it is necessary, before the siege arrives, to be well provided with food.

Protect your chip stack. If you allow your stack to dwindle, you will begin to play with fear, at which point you are guaranteed to lose.

MACHIAVELLI SAID:
One ought to take care not to be...forced to capitulate to assaults. [I]t has been said that one ought to guard against the first onrush. If this onrush is withstood, then only with difficulty will you be over-come.

Do not let opponents bully you. Take a stand the first time, and opponents will hesitate to bully you in the future.

MACHIAVELLI SAID:
The besieged ought to use more diligence in how they guard them-selves when the enemy is distant than when he is near. And they ought to guard those places better that they think can be attacked less...because either they believe the place is strong or they believe it is inaccessible.

Be wary of traps. Your opponent can feign weakness as easily as you can. Do not get overconfident when you have a strong hand. Unless you have the nuts, you are never invincible. Always try to determine the likely hands your opponent may be playing.

MACHIAVELLI SAID:
What benefits the enemy, harms you, and what benefits you, harms
the enemy.

While this maxim may seem simple and obvious, implementing it is difficult and complex. Every move you make should be made only after careful consideration of this maxim. Betting or raising when you have the best
of it benefits you and harms your opponent since you are the favorite to
win the pot. It does not matter who eventually wins the hand. So long as
you consistently make moves that benefit you, you will win in the end.
For instance, if you are playing seven card stud and are on a draw, try raising on fourth street in order to get your opponents to check on fifth street
when the bet is double. If an opponent checks on fifth street when he is
the favorite, this benefits you and harms him. Every bet, raise, check, or
call should be considered in the context of whether it benefits you. For example, you should only put more money in the pot either if you are the favorite or if it gives you the opportunity to win the pot right there when
your opponent is vulnerable.

In addition, every card should be considered in the context of the overall game. For instance, say you are playing hold'em and you are dealt a
pair of Jacks. You raise and both the small and big blind call. The flop
comes 9♥, 10♣, 4♣. You bet your overpair and both of the other players call. The turn brings J♣. Both players check and you eagerly bet
with your new set. To your surprise, you are immediately raised and re-
raised. In your delight in hitting your set, you completely overlooked
how that same J♣ may have helped your opponents. While you
thought that J♣ was a good card for you, it is in reality a very dangerous card in that it may have improved your opponents more than it
helped you.

Likely, hands your opponents could be holding include K-Q, or any
two clubs. That J♣ would improve any of those hands to a better hand
than yours. Any card that helps your opponent more than it helps you is
harmful to you, not beneficial. If you had taken the time to implement the
preceding maxim prior to acting in this situation, you would have
checked and taken a free card to see if you could hit a full house or quads.

Instead, you must now decide whether to call two bets (for a total of three) with a hand that is almost assuredly behind right now.

Always consider how every card dealt affects every player at the table. Say you are playing seven card stud and one of the players receives the 10♦ on fifth street pairing his door card. While this card obviously helps this player, it may hurt two other players' chances for a diamond flush and King-high straight, respectively.

> **MACHIAVELLI SAID:**
> Whoever is more vigilant in observing the designs of the enemy
> in war, and endures much hardship in training his army, will incur
> fewer dangers and can have greater hope for victory.

Closely observe your opponents. Whenever you can put your opponent on a hand, you benefit. No matter how carefully you study your opponents, you will always suffer defeat. Losing hands is a fact of life for any poker player. How well you handle losing will go a long way in determining your success at the poker table. Most decent players can play good cards reasonably well. Where the great poker players separate themselves is in their ability to play well when the cards are running bad for them. The ability to minimize losses (or even eke out some wins) and to maintain your composure in these situations is critical to success.

> **MACHIAVELLI SAID:**
> Never lead your soldiers into an engagement … unless you see
> hope for victory.

Do not squander chips. Do not employ them if you do not perceive an advantage. The great thing about poker is that there will be a new hand dealt in just a few short minutes. Have patience. Do not play marginal hands just because you want to play.

MACHIAVELLI SAID:
No course of action is better than that which you have concealed
from the enemy until the time you have executed it.

Conceal your moves and intentions at the table. Do everything within
your power to keep your opponents from figuring out your play.

MACHIAVELLI SAID:
To know how to recognize an opportunity in war, and take it,
benefits you more than anything else.

If you only play strong hands, you will not be a very successful player. You
may not lose many hands, but you will not get much action from your opponents when you do play. When you do get action, you will likely be up
against a strong hand. To be a winning poker player, you must exploit your
opponents' vulnerabilities. When you sense your opponent is vulnerable,
it does not matter what cards you are holding. Attack and seize the pot.

MACHIAVELLI SAID:
Nature creates few men brave; industry and training makes many.

Sitting down to a poker table in a casino can be a nerve-racking experience for many beginning players—even for those with plenty of online or
home-game experience. Just remember that everyone else is playing with
the same deck as you are. Play your game and maintain your discipline,
and you will do fine.

MACHIAVELLI SAID:
Discipline in war counts more than fury.

Poker is a competition, but it is not football or boxing. You do not gain
anything by unleashing your fury on your opponent. Instead, you will go

on tilt, and your opponents will be quick to take advantage. Maintain your discipline. Minimizing your mistakes is as important as exploiting your opponents' mistakes.

MACHIAVELLI SAID:
It is better in organizing an engagement to reserve great aid behind the front line than to spread out your soldiers to make a greater front.

Employ your chips wisely. Do not call many bets in order to play more hands. It is much better to play fewer hands and play them with strength than to play many hands with weakness. Save your chips to use when you can be the aggressor.

MACHIAVELLI SAID:
New and speedy things frighten armies, while the customary and slow things are appreciated little by them; you will therefore make your army experienced and learn the strength of a new enemy by skirmishes, before you come to an engagement with him.

Do not be quick to engage your opponent before you have had ample opportunity to size him up. Test, probe, and observe before committing a large number of chips to a pot with an unknown opponent.

MACHIAVELLI SAID:
Whoever pursues a routed enemy in a disorganized manner does nothing but become vanquished from having been a victor.

Do not let winning make you overconfident or even reckless. Attack short stacks and take advantage of scared money. However, do so in a disciplined manner in order to keep your opponents from getting back in the game.

MACHIAVELLI SAID:
Whoever does not make provisions necessary to live is overcome
without protection.

Play within your means so that you always have enough chips to defend
your hands when necessary.

MACHIAVELLI SAID:
Change your course of action when you become aware that the
enemy has foreseen it.

Consistently mix up your play in order to keep your play unpredictable.

MACHIAVELLI SAID:
Counsel with many on the things you ought to do, and confer with
few on what you do afterward.

Discuss strategy with those whose opinion you trust, but avoid sharing
your secrets with many.

MACHIAVELLI SAID:
Good captains never come to an engagement unless necessity
compels them or the opportunity calls them.

Do not enter a pot unless you have a good reason to do so. A good reason
is that you perceive an advantage or your hand is so good that you must
play even when you suspect your opponent may be strong as well.

MACHIAVELLI SAID:
Act so your enemies do not know how you want to organize your
army for battle.

Hide your intentions. Do not always bet the same way in the same situation.

MACHIAVELLI SAID:
Accidents are remedied with difficulty unless you think quickly.

Whether you make a mistake or suffer a setback, adjust quickly to the new situation in order to avoid compounding the mistake.

MACHIAVELLI SAID:
Men, steel, money, and bread are the sinews of war; but of these four, the first two are more necessary, for men and steel find money and bread, but money and bread do not find men and steel. The unarmed rich man is the prize of the poor soldier.

A player who possesses virtù will always find a way to win chips. A player without virtu will not succeed no matter how many chips he starts with.

MACHIAVELLI SAID:
I would have enlarged it with glory, or I would have lost it without shame.

If you are going to play poker, give yourself the chance to win. Play to win. Do not play not to lose. Exercise virtù. Be a Prince. Do not go down without a fight.

XI

Machiavellian Tournament Strategy

Tournament poker is an entirely different game from ring games and, thus, requires a different strategy. While the fundamentals of Machiavellian poker strategy are still applicable, there are some critical differences that are worth mentioning. For purposes of this discussion, I have limited the analysis to tournaments that may last for a few hours and to blinds or antes that raise every 15–30 minutes. These tournaments move quickly and one must adjust his play. For tournaments that last longer such as five-day championship events, the analysis would be much different, especially for the beginning stages of such tournaments when survival is a primary goal of the participants.

Si guarda al fine.

In tournament poker, as in ring games, one looks to the result. The difference with tournament poker is that the outcome comes a lot quicker. Whenever you are eliminated, you will know where you stand. You will either be in the money or out of the money. You will know exactly what place you finished in out of exactly how many entrants. You are judged by how high you finish in the tournament. Since most tournaments take hours, not days or months, and you can be eliminated at any time, judgment is always right around the corner. In no limit tournaments, judgment can literally be one hand away at any point in the game.

With this in mind, how should you play a tournament? By using all your Machiavellian skills. However, you must adjust to the situation. When playing in a tournament, once you are out of chips, you are done. You cannot reach into your pocket to buy more chips. The blinds or antes or both increase quickly, significantly altering the game. As players are eliminated, tables are consolidated, and you constantly find yourself playing with new faces just as you are getting a read on opponents and establishing your dominance at the table. You must be aware of every other player's stack size. Short stacks may not necessarily be scared money. While you should attack short stacks, they must make a play before they are blinded or anted out. Thus, they are apt to engage with any playable hand.

Tournament play requires a much greater and more delicate balance between chip preservation and chip accumulation. In tournaments, chip preservation now means survival. You cannot squander chips. You cannot afford to test opponents. It is not worthwhile since your chips are too valuable and there is a good chance you will only be playing with a particular opponent for a short period. You cannot afford to play pot odds. Again, your chips are too valuable to waste when you are a 5–1 underdog, even though you are getting 7–1 odds to play. You are judged by your result in this tournament only. Every chip you have takes on added importance since it is crucial to your survival.

However, you must balance survival with chip accumulation. Since the betting levels in tournaments rise rather quickly, you must accumulate chips consistently in order to maintain a chip stack of adequate force. While you do not want to squander chips, you must be more aggressive. You must take advantage of every opportunity. You must play disciplined, but you will need to force the action at times. You will not have the luxury of waiting for the perfect opportunity or until you know your opponents as well as you know yourself. Do everything in your power to understand the situation and your opponent and then go with your gut. Implement your chips with maximum force. Play with strength. Take charge from the outset. Be a Prince.

Be a Prince.

Tournaments move quickly. Thus, your ascension to power must be accelerated. You must play with a sense of urgency. You must be willing to battle and defeat your opponent from the beginning. If you sense weakness, attack. Do not wait for the perfect moment. To do so invites failure. That moment may never come. By the time you have the perfect read on your opponent, your table may be broken up.

Play with confidence. Assume you are the strongest player at your table. Play one table at a time. Be the leader of your table. No matter how many players are entered into the tournament, at any given time you only have to outplay the opponents at your table. When your table is broken up and you join an existing table, do not be hesitant. Again, assume you are the strongest player at the table. Establish your dominance. You may think you are at a disadvantage since you do not know these new opponents, but they do not know you either. Study and learn and keep abreast of the situation, but you do not have the luxury of time. Any perceived opportunity must be acted on.

You must be the one who dictates the terms of play. The first one to act, often wins the pot. This is particularly true in no limit tournaments or the later stages of limit tournaments. So many good starting hands in no limit hold'em have an approximate 50 percent chance of winning heads-up against another good starting hand. It is much easier to be on the offensive rather than the defensive in those situations.

For example, say you are in the later stages of a no limit hold'em tournament in which the blinds and antes are well worth winning pre-flop. You find yourself in middle position with a pair of eights. You have an average chip stack, and while others at the table have you *covered*, they would be short-stacked if they lost an all-in bet to you. If you make a big raise or even go all-in, you put tremendous pressure on the opponents yet to act. Any players holding two overcards would have a hard time calling your bet knowing that they would, in all likelihood, have an approximate 50 percent chance at best. Even players holding a pair of nines, tens, and, possibly, even Jacks would be hesitant to call. They know that if you are AK or AQ, they are only a slight favorite, and if you have a higher pair than they do, they are a huge underdog. This puts a tremendous amount of pressure on them to call. The only hands that are sure to call you are AA, KK, and, most likely, QQ. The odds of the few remaining players having one of those hands are certainly possible but not likely.

Thus, by betting first, you greatly increase your chances of winning the pot without a challenge. It is much easier to bet a 50/50 hand than to call it. Think of it this way. If you had those same eights in late position and a player in middle position went all-in, what would you do? You would have to fold them. The best-case scenario for you would be to be up against two overcards, which would only make you a slight favorite. However, if you are up against a higher pair, you are a big underdog. The risk is just too big to call here.

Now, let us go back to the original scenario in which you are first to act in middle position with a pair of eights. This time, you only make a small raise. Now, a player behind you raises all-in. Unbeknownst to you, he has AQ. If you had gone all-in in the first place, it is highly likely this player would have folded. Now, you are forced to decide whether it is worth risking all your chips when you are at best a slight favorite. In any event, you are guaranteed a showdown if you call.

Play with strength. While it may seem counterintuitive, it is often less risky to bet more chips than less. You cannot play with the fear that your opponent may have a monster hand. He might, and there will be times when you bet into a monster and get burned. That is poker. However, if you always play with fear, you are giving up your biggest weapon, which is the ability to put your opponent on the defensive. I cannot emphasize enough how important a concept this is.

To illustrate this concept, I would like to offer an example from a recent no limit hold'em tournament I participated in. I was eliminated early in this tournament, but my friend (let us call him Steve) advanced to the final table. This particular tournament started with sixty-six players and only paid the top four. A $50 buy-in with rebuys and an add-on occurred in the first hour of play. Most players had about $150 invested in the tournament, and as this tournament was a super satellite, the top three places received $2,600 vouchers into a much bigger tournament and fourth place received $2,450 in cash. Fifth place received nothing. This created an interesting and tense final table. One had to be careful not to risk all his chips. Yet, so long as you finished in the top four, it did not matter how many chips you had left.

Once the table was down to five players, my friend Steve limps in from middle position with A, 8 off-suit. Not a real strong hand, but Steve has about $50,000 ($48,000 after limping in) in chips and is one of the chip leaders. The blinds are $1,000–$2,000 with $500 antes. Everyone folds to the big blind (let us call him Player OTB for *on the bubble*). The big blind has $27,500 in chips left. He has K, Q off-suit, and he raises Steve $10,000. Steve calmly looks the situation over and asks Player OTB how many chips he has left. Player OTB answers he has $17,500 left. If Steve calls here, he will have about $38,000 in chips left, but if he raises Player OTB all-in and Player OTB calls, then Steve will have only about $20,000 in chips left.

At these levels and at this point in the tournament, that is a big difference. However, if Steve calls, he lets Player OTB see the flop, and Player OTB will be the first to act after the flop. Even if the flop brings an ace, Steve will have a hard time calling a bet with his weak kicker. However, if Steve raises Player OTB prior to the flop, he puts Player OTB in a very precarious position. Player OTB has to decide if he wants to risk everything on this hand. If Player OTB loses, he goes home empty-handed. Even though it is less costly to Steve to call rather than raise, a call here carries much greater risk. It will be very difficult for Steve to win the pot if he calls, and Steve will end up losing another $10,000 in chips. In my opinion, Steve's only choices here are either to fold or to re-raise Player OTB all-in.

Steve decides to re-raise Player OTB all-in. It is a brilliant move. Player OTB know that Steve does not have a strong hand since Steve originally limped in. Yet, Player OTB knows that any hand that Steve is holding could easily end up beating his. As much as Player OTB wants to call, he realizes that he cannot risk it at this point in the tournament. The primary goal at this moment is survival. The $17,500 in chips that Player OTB still has are plenty to work with in order to stay alive while he waits out one more elimination. The $2,450 difference between fourth and fifth place is too great. Thus, Player OTB folds, and Steve picks up a nice pot to take the chip lead and leaves an opponent short-stacked.

This was only Steve's third tournament ever. However, he is a quick

learner. It did not take him long to realize the value of putting your opponent on the defensive. By being the aggressor, Steve established himself as
the Prince of the table. He was going to dictate the terms. He implemented
his chips to maximum force. Steve had enough chips to withstand a hit
but he knew that Player OTB did not. Steve adeptly exploited this dispar-
ity. After this hand, Steve maintained control of the table and was easily
the chip leader when the tournament ended, once there were three players remaining. Player OTB found himself with approximately the same
amount of chips as another short stack at the table after this hand. Those
two players worked out a deal that if one of them was eliminated next, the
other would give him $1,000 out of his winnings. With the pressure now
off, Player OTB was eliminated quickly thereafter in fifth place. Yet, walking away with $1,000 in his pocket was a lot better than going home
empty-handed.

One mistake in tournament play can be fatal. You do not have the luxury of being able to reach into your pocket and buy more chips. You must
be on your game at all times. You cannot play scared and you cannot be
afraid to lose. You must be patient and disciplined but still play with a
sense of urgency. In order to survive, you cannot fear elimination. Be
proactive. Give yourself a chance to win. Your overall tournament success
will be greatly enhanced if you take a chance while you still have the force
of your chips rather than waiting for the perfect opportunity. Do not allow
yourself to be blinded down to the point where your chips have lost all
their force and you are sure to get a caller no matter what you do. Exercise
all the elements of virtu from the moment the tournament starts.

Virtù

Remember, for Machiavelli virtù was a collective embodiment of courage,
intellect, cunning, skill, determination, resiliency, ambition, toughness,
ability, and prowess. While these traits are essential no matter what form
of poker you are playing, they must be implemented immediately and
constantly in a tournament. Every hand is critical in a tournament, and you
cannot afford to let your guard down for one second. Every hand and
every move must be played for maximum profit whether that means fold-

ing, calling, checking, or raising. You cannot take time off. You must observe every player every hand. You must know the situation at all times. Know how soon the blinds or antes will raise and what the next level of betting will be. Know how many players are still left in the tournament and what the average chip stack is. Know who is short-stacked at your table. Know if your table is likely to be broken up soon. Know how many more players must be eliminated before you are in the money. Knowledge is power. Since the essence of poker is that each player has limited knowledge in every hand, you must make sure that you at least are aware of every bit of knowledge available to you.

Be courageous with your knowledge. In tournament play, you will have to act whenever you perceive a weakness or opportunity. You will not always be correct, and there will be times when you are correct and still lose. However, tournaments do not reward ultraconservative play. Tournaments reward courageous, disciplined play.

Be cunning. Just as you must act on every perceived advantage, so must your opponents in order to advance. Do not give your opponents that opportunity against you. Mix up your play. Be the player no one wants to engage in a pot. Attempt a few aggressive unorthodox plays early on to establish your unpredictability.

Do not give up in a tournament. Everyone has heard the stories about how all you need is "a chip and a chair" to win the tournament. Yet, in reality, few players take this mantra to heart. Once short-stacked, they give up and just throw in their chips. Do not give up. Jack Strauss memorably won the *World Series of Poker No Limit Hold'em Championship* in 1982 after at one time being down to one chip. Sure, he had to have some luck. Every tournament winner does. But he also had a tremendous amount of skill, and he never gave up on that skill.

I have seen the following scenario in tournaments countless times, and I never understand the thinking. Player A has about $4,000 in chips when the average stack is about $8,000. Player B has $10,000 in chips. Player B bets $3,500 pre-flop and Player A calls. Everyone else folds. After the flop, Player B checks and Player A throws in his last $500. Why? Player B is virtually guaranteed to call no matter what. Why risk that last $500? Unless you have the absolute nuts, it is simply not worth it. If Player B is willing to let you survive, then take advantage of it. Player B is, in my opinion, making a big mistake by not putting you all-in. Yet, so many times I see Player A make this bet only to lose to Player B. Every chip has value in a tournament. While Player A certainly would need some luck to survive with $500, anyone who has played the game can attest to the whims of Fortune. With high antes and blinds, one win can get a player right back in the game. You should be playing the game because you have skill. So long as you are alive, you give yourself the opportunity to use that skill.

Think about the consequence of every bet you make. If you are playing seven card stud, with two pair, and it is obvious your opponent is on a flush draw, then check if it is your turn to act first on the river. Why bet here? If your opponent hits his flush, he will raise you. If he misses, he will fold. You have nothing to gain but an extra bet to lose by betting out. By checking, you may even induce a bluff attempt by your opponent, giving you the chance to win another bet. Every extra chip you win or save is critical in tournament play. You must exercise virtù with every move you make.

You are playing to compete. Even if you are a recreational player, you must use every ounce of resiliency, determination, and toughness in order to compete. Tournaments are competitive and full of traps. You will cross paths with many different players and styles in a short period. There is only one way to deal with all these contrasting players and styles. You must use your prowess. You must be the one to dictate the terms of play. You must control the action. To do otherwise leaves much too much to uncertainty. Use every aspect of virtù to lessen the impact of Fortune.

Fortune

While Fortune is no more capricious in tournament play than ring games, her effect can be disastrous in tournament play. One bad beat can mean elimination. In addition, due to the nature of tournament play, players will turn to Fortune to help them out. Recently, I was playing a no limit hold'em tournament when the following hand took place. I had about $3,000 in chips, and the blinds were $100–$200 with $25 antes. I was in middle position and everyone folded to me. I looked at my cards and saw A♦, Q♦. I raised to $600, which was slightly more than the $550 in the pot. Everyone folded to the big blind. The big blind had exactly $400 left—just enough to call. Let us call this player Player SS (for short stack). Player SS looked at his cards and then thought aloud. He knew if he called, he would have to win, or he would be eliminated. He also knew that he faced the small blind next, and with the antes at $25 each, he could be *blinded out* in a short period. But he also did not have very good cards.

Player SS looked at me and said, "You want me to call." Then he asked if I would be upset if he called and then drew out on me. I did not respond either time. Finally, Player SS called with 8, 10 off-suit, knowing that he would be behind me. He reasoned, however, that he would need some luck sometime, and going in now with a mediocre hand heads-up when he could win a nice pot was as good a time as any. Of course, he flopped a 10, I never improved, and he won a nice pot to get him right back in the game.

While I am not sure that I would have made the same call as he did in that situation, I cannot fault Player SS for the play he made. He decided he would rather make a stand than risk being blinded out. Even though he did not have a great hand, he knew he would be heads-up. Furthermore, even though he knew he was behind, unless I had a pair of 10's or higher, he would not be that big of an underdog.

The point of this scenario is not to showcase a bad beat or gather sympathy for myself. Rather, it is to illustrate how players will often play a hand in tournament play that they otherwise would not (in a ring game), knowing they will need some luck. In the previous scenario, if Player SS had a few more chips, he would not make that call and I would have won the pot uncontested. But that is tournament poker. I found it very telling that Player SS asked if I would be upset if he happened to draw out on me. Not that it would affect his decision, but I think he was used to seeing players get upset when they were outdrawn in hands, and he wanted the entire table to understand why he was going in. (I am sure he was also trying to get a tell on me.)

Now, certainly, I was not happy that I had lost that hand, but I did not let it affect my play. About half an hour later, I was moved to another table, and the blinds had increased to $300–$600 and the antes were $100. With ten players per table, it would now cost each player $1,900 a round. I had a below-average stack of about $3,000. I knew I still had enough force to chase other players out, but I also knew that my force would diminish quickly if I did not scoop some pots.

I was on the button when everyone folded to me. I looked at my cards and saw K♣, J♣ and went all-in. The small blind immediately called and the big blind folded. The small blind (let us call him Player AA) had me covered with about $1,000 to spare, and he turned over a pair of aces. I stood up at the table and waited for the inevitable. However, I received a K on the flop, another K on the turn and a blank on the river. I was still alive. Well, Player AA was absolutely hysterical at the injustice he just experienced. He made some rude comments to me questioning how I could have played such a hand. I bit my tongue instead of reminding him that I bet out with K, J suited; I did not call an all-in bet with it. I just as soon let Player AA stay mad and go on tilt. Sure enough, the very next hand, I had a pair of tens. I made a medium raise, and Player AA calls all-in from the button. Everyone else folds, and Player AA turns over 9, 7 off-suit and is eliminated when he does not receive any further help. I went on to finish in the money. So did Player SS. Player AA obviously did not.

In every poker tournament, there will be many hands when players face elimination, and it is up to Fortune whether they survive or not. Every player will be eliminated except one. And the odds are that the winner will have survived an elimination hand at some point during the tournament. In this particular tournament, both Player SS and I could very easily have been eliminated without making the money. On the other hand, while Player AA suffered a bad beat, he eliminated himself by giving up afterward.

You can only control what you can control in a tournament. The best defense against Fortune is to accumulate chips early, so you have everyone else at your table covered. You want to avoid being all-in against an opponent with more chips. Recognize that short stacks have an incentive to go all-in unless they are on the bubble. Do not get upset no matter what Fortune brings to the table. Always play the situation.

If you are short-stacked, play that stack for optimum value. Skillful players have a slight edge over their opponents when both are getting cards. However, skillful players have a much larger edge over their opponents in how they play when things are not going their way. Realize that at some point during the tournament you will face elimination. When the time happens, do not fear Fortune but face her head on. In the interim, do everything in your power to delay that hand when you face elimination. Exercise free will.

Free Will

One of the biggest obstacles ring players face when they try their hands at tournament play is being proactive. I see it happen all the time. A player freezes waiting for that opportune time to play a hand. In the interim, he slowly bleeds to death as the blinds and antes eat away at his stack. Finally, he is down to his last chip, which he throws in for a forced blind and must take whatever cards come his way when there are sure to be a couple of callers. Whether he wins that particular hand or not is irrelevant. He is sure to be eliminated once the blinds or antes rise.

A ring player who does not adjust his game for tournament play will never advance to the money. He will probably advance to the middle of the pack every time but never further. The reason being is that the ring player who does not adjust will not feel the sense of urgency. He will be content to wait out dry spells and bad starting cards. He will not push the action until he sees a clear opportunity. Even if this ring player plays a solid, tight, aggressive game suitable for ring games, it will only advance him so far in a tournament. The levels rise too fast in tournament play. You do not have the luxury of waiting for the perfect opportunity to present itself. In a ring game, you can practice a great deal of patience until you get a proper read on your opponents, and it will not cost you a lot of money. Tournaments move too quickly for that strategy. In most nightly tournaments, the levels will increase every twenty minutes. Within two hours, you are up to the seventh level. In tournament play, the faster the blinds rise, the greater the role of Fortune. You must be proactive early. It is simply too costly to play a patient game.

Fortunately, you do not have to play a patient game. You have free will. Exercise it. Play position. Play marginal hands when you need a win. Be the first one to make a play for the pot even if you do not have a hand. Play scare cards as if they helped you. Do something. If you sense weakness, pounce on it. If you sense vulnerability, attack. Do not wait until you are 100 percent sure. Do not wait for cards. Do not expect your opponents to give you a hand if you do not go for it.

Most importantly, implement your chips while they still have force. In a no limit hold'em tournament, it is much better to make a big bet with a marginal hand than to wait too long for a strong hand to play. By the time you get that strong hand, if you are left with insufficient force, you are sure to get callers. In addition, even if you win with that strong hand, you will still be left short-stacked and with limited force.

So how do you know what is a short stack? In most tournaments, the casino will keep a running count of remaining players. If you know how many players started, you should be able to figure out easily what the average stack is of the remaining players. Since your ultimate goal is to keep advancing, you would like to have at least an average stack. If you fall below the average, be alert and realize that you will have to start looking more aggressively for opportunities. Once you fall below an average stack, there will be a majority of players who have you covered. This puts you in a vulnerable position, as there will be more players willing to take you on. You can still inflict damage, however, so do not panic. If you are playing hold'em, there is no need to get flustered so long as your stack is equal to at least ten times the amount of the big blind. However, keep abreast of the situation. Know when the blinds will increase and to how much. For example, say the current level is $50–$100 blinds with no ante and you have $1,000 in chips. You think you are in decent shape. However, in two minutes, the blinds will increase to $75–150 with $25 antes. Assuming ten players are at your table, in two minutes a round of poker will increase from $150 to $475. This is a big difference. All of a sudden, that $1,000 stack looks quite vulnerable.

Stay ahead of the game and be prepared. As players tend to tighten up once the levels increase, think about making a play for the pot with the first hand of the new level. Remember you have a choice. With a lot of money in the pot, you can make a play for it. If you have force, you can choose to use it. When you use force and put your opponent on the defensive, you make it very difficult for him to call. A hand he would otherwise have played, he now folds. A very playable hand becomes a marginal call. Opponents can only afford to call significant force with very strong hands. If an opponent does have a strong hand, he is likely to raise rather than call in that situation if he is a good player who knows how to use his chips. If a strong player calls a big bet after the flop, be wary of a trap.

The most important asset a poker player has is his chips. To let that asset slip away without even playing a hand is the most wasteful and foolish thing a poker player can do in a tournament. To squander your force is to lose your ability to exercise free will. If you allow your chip stack to be blinded off, you lose your free will. You will be forced to play whatever cards you are dealt, and every opponent will know it. Think about it. Take the recent example in which you have $1,000 and the blinds have just increased to $75–$150 with $25 antes. You are in middle position with Q, 9 suited and everyone folds to you. If you bet $600, you stand an excellent chance of winning a $475 pot uncontested. Even if you are called, you have outs. If you are raised, you can fold and still have $400. Instead, you decide to wait for a strong hand. You finally get 99 when you are down to $225 in chips, and you go all-in. You are sure to get at least one caller. While neither scenario is ideal, between the two, which situation would you rather be in? I think the first scenario is clearly preferable because you are playing from a position of power. You have two chances to win the pot: First, you can win it uncontested. If you get a caller, you still have a chance to make a hand. In the second situation, not only will you surely get a caller, but you will still be short-stacked and facing an uphill battle if you win the pot.

To paraphrase Machiavelli, play to enlarge your chip stack with glory or lose it without shame. In tournament play, every player will be eliminated except one. There is no shame in being eliminated unless you go out without a fight. It is far better to make a play from a position of power than to be forced into a last stand from a position of weakness.

Power

In tournament power, there is no room for weakness. There is no room for hesitation. There is no room for indecisiveness. You cannot be equivocal in tournament play. You must act boldly, and when you play, you must play with strength. Do these things, and you will ascend to power at the table.

The majority of tournaments you play will last anywhere from three to six hours. These tournaments move quickly and are a real Machiavellian test. Players with virtu who establish their dominance are rewarded. Leaders advance, followers are eliminated. No matter how many players are entered into the tournament, you only need to play one table at a time. Establish your dominance at the table you are playing. These are your opponents. You must treat them as subjects under your command. You want to control the action. You want to dictate the terms of play. You want to be the one everyone else fears. You want to be the chip leader.

In tournaments, it is critical to establish yourself as the leader of the table as soon as possible for a number of different reasons: First, there is a tremendous advantage in being the chip leader of your table. You can afford to be more aggressive. Other players will avoid challenging you. You can attack smaller stacks. Second, in tournament play tables are constantly consolidated. As you advance, you will often be moved to other tables. Even if your table is not broken up, new players will come to your table as opponents are eliminated. The composition of your table will always be in a state of flux. As such, you will need to maintain your position of power or even be forced to reestablish it, throughout the tournament. You cannot let up at all. Play with a Machiavellian purpose throughout. Finally, the betting levels in tournament play increase quickly. You cannot afford to be too patient. While you must balance your competing goals of survival and chip accumulation, you cannot afford to be passive. If you are going to play, you must be aggressive. In the later rounds when the levels are expensive, avoid limping in. If you are going to play, control the action. Be the first one to make a play for the pot. By being the aggressor, you put your opponents on the defensive. When they are on the defensive, they are easier to read.

The power of a large chip stack cannot be understated. If you are forced to change tables and arrive at your new seat with the biggest stack at the table, you will automatically be respected and feared. The fact that you possess the largest stack in and of itself provides you with power.

Remember that the effectiveness of any bet or raise you make depends on the effect it has on your opponent—not the effect it has on you. If you have a small stack, a bet that you may consider large would probably be considered small to a much larger stack. When you are the chip leader, it is much easier to make bets or raises that will effectively put your opponent on the defensive. Whenever you make a bet or raise, consider how much to bet based on the effect it is likely to have on your opponent. You must consider, among other things, the size of the pot, the size of your opponent's chip stack, the stage of the tournament, and your opponent's position.

Tournament play requires strong decisive play. You want to be the large stack against your opponents' short stacks. Large stacks have a tremendous advantage while short stacks play with extreme vulnerability. Follow your Machiavellian strategy to establish your dominance. As you ascend to power and seek to retain it, remember to implement statesmanship.

Statesmanship

Even a short stack can do damage in tournament play. You want to preserve your chips, and you do not want other players gunning for you. Inexperienced players tend to get more upset in tournament play than ring games. They blame others for their mistakes. They become antagonistic when they are in danger of being eliminated. I have seen players slow play aces when they have a short stack and the blinds and antes are high. They limp in, allow for a couple of callers, and then get quite ticked off when an opponent flops two pair. They fail to recognize that they never should have let that opponent see the flop. Once they lose such a hand, these players are likely to blame the winner of the pot for their mistake. Sensing elimination, they will go after the perceived culprit rather than trying to build their stack back up. They figure they are not going to finish in the money anyway, so they might as well exact some revenge.

What can you do to avoid these attacks? Practice statesmanship. Never criticize your opponent. Encourage their mistakes. Downplay your wins. Inform them that there is a lot of luck in tournaments. Control the action while maintaining the peace. While Machiavelli recognizes that it is better to be feared than loved, be a benevolent dictator. Gain the respect and fear of your opponents.

As a statesman, have a thorough understanding of the geography and history of your table. Know who is likely to defend blinds and who is not. Know how each player is likely to play a short stack. Some players get extremely aggressive with short stacks, while others completely tighten up. Know what stage of the tournament you are in. If there are only a few more eliminations to go until the remaining players are in the money, most short stacks will tighten up. Take advantage of that. Once the short stacks reach the money, they are likely to get aggressive, as they now feel they have nothing to lose and they want to take a shot at accumulating chips.

It is important as a statesman to use position. Position is critical in tournament play—especially in the later expensive rounds. In no limit hold'em tournaments, it becomes critical to win at least one pot per round in order to avoid being blinded out. Since you cannot rely on getting cards, you must rely on position. If everyone folds to you in late position, you must seriously consider making a play for the pot regardless of what you are holding. In the later rounds of no limit hold'em, very few hands ever see the flop. That is because someone will usually make a strong play for the pot making it very difficult to call unless you hold a very strong hand. As a tactical strategy, consider making a play for the pot from early position. There are a couple of reasons for doing this: First, you have the chance to be the first one to make a play for the pot when you are the one acting first. (You will not always get a chance to make a play for the pot from late position because an opponent acting before you may make a play.) Next, when you bet big from early position, your opponents are more likely to give you credit for a strong hand.

If you are playing stud, take advantage of high cards. If you get to lead the betting, then by all means bet. You will have a very good opportunity to lead for a couple of streets, and you stand a very good chance of being able to represent top pair and chase out opponents. In the more expensive rounds, opponents are less likely to chase drawing hands, and they will respect high cards.

No matter what the game, drawing hands become less playable in the later, more expensive rounds. Not only will it be expensive to chase draws, but most hands will be played with few players, making draws unprofitable. If you are heads-up and you sense your opponent is on a draw, attack to keep him from chasing.

Human Nature

No matter what strategy you implement, know your opponent. Tournaments require bold, powerful play. It is much easier to be aggressive when you know your opponents. You do not want to play in a vacuum. You must balance survival against chip accumulation. You do not want to be aggressive for the sake of being aggressive. You do not want to play aggressively in hopes that your opponents will notice. Rather, you want to be aggressive in the context of the game. Specifically, you want to be aggressive when it will pay off for you.

Study your opponent. Know his tendencies and see how he is adapting. Most tournament players will adjust their play as the levels increase. When the rounds get expensive, players rarely limp in. If they are going to play, they play with strength. If you get someone limping in front of you in the expensive rounds, they are vulnerable, and you will stand an excellent chance of being able to chase them out with aggressive play.

Many players just want to finish in the money. Winning the entire tournament is secondary. These players will completely tighten up when they are on the bubble. These players will fold everything but aces when they are only a few eliminations away from placing in the money. They do not care if they only have one chip left so long as they are in the money. Take advantage of this. Challenge players when they tighten up. Pick up antes and blinds. Know which opponents are playing to win and which are just hoping to survive. Understand their goals and the tactics they will use to accomplish them. Understand their nature.

Understanding your opponent is only half the battle. Know your own nature. What type of player are you? Are you naturally aggressive? Then use that to your advantage to try to build a chip lead. However, make sure to temper that aggressiveness when you need to. A few years back, I played a super satellite where the top six players would receive a seat in a

larger tournament. One player (let us call him Player Hyper) was super aggressive and had built up a tremendous stack by the time we were down
to twelve players. At this point in the game, all Player Hyper had to do was
sit back, and he was guaranteed to win a seat. He had enough chips to
post the blinds and antes, fold every hand and still finish in the top six.
The tournament would end once we were down to six players, so there
was no first place prize to shoot for. Well, Player Hyper could not help
himself. He could not temper his play, and he continued his super aggressive ways, which proved fatal in the face of smart, disciplined opponents
looking for any opportunity to exploit to help them advance. Player Hyper
went out in ninth place cursing his bad luck. While he only had himself
to blame, Player Hyper could never see that. He knew only one way to
play, and he was incapable of looking within himself to see how he could
improve.

On the other hand, if you are a patient player who lets the game come
to you, then play your game with a close eye on the situation. Be ready to
step up and force the action if you are in danger of being short-stacked.
Take advantage of your conservative image by being situationally aggressive.

Know your goals. If you are a beginning player, you may very well be
content to just advance far or finish in the money. However, if your goal is
to win the tournament, then play to win. To finish first, you must avoid
falling too far behind at any point in time. Play smart and disciplined but
give yourself the chance to win. Attack those players who are content to
just finish in the money. Exploit players who are more concerned with
survival than chip accumulation.

Art of War

Adopt your military mind-set before the tournament begins. Preparedness
leads to victory, so do as much preparation beforehand as you can. Make
sure you are well rested and mentally ready to go. Check out the schedule
ahead of time. Ask for a timetable of when (and how much) the blinds or
antes will increase. Know when the breaks are and plan accordingly. If
you will not have a break for hours, then make sure you have eaten ahead

of time. Go to the bathroom before the tournament starts. Have single dollar bills to tip the waitstaff for drinks. Think of everything you can so that you have minimal distractions during the tournament.

Prepare a tactical strategy. Determine ahead of time how many chips you must win per hour to maintain a healthy stack at each level. Figure out how conservative you can be before you face any danger of being blinded or anted out. Get to your table ahead of time. Tournaments typically always start on time, and if players are late, their chips will be blinded or anted in turn. Take advantage of these empty seats. Talk to your opponents before the tournament starts to get a feel for their experience level and expectations. Are they seasoned veterans? Are they just there to play a tournament because they have seen them on television and they want to be able to tell their friends about the experience?

Once the tournament starts, be in your military mind-set. Your civilian self should have been abandoned before you sat down to the table. Be ready to attack at any time. While you will not be attacking all the time, you must be prepared to attack at any moment in order to take advantage of any opportunity. In tournament play, you cannot afford to miss any opportunity. While one such mistake may appear to be harmless, it can ultimately prove to be your downfall. Say you fail to win $500 early on. Later when you are short-stacked and go all-in, that extra $500 could have been the difference in forcing an opponent out. Your antennae must be up at all times. Stay in tune with the game. Study your opponents. Wait until it is your turn to act before making a decision so that you have the advantage of having every available piece of information in order to make an informed decision.

Have no reservations at the poker table. You are only judged by how far you advance, and it is up to you how you choose to get there. Do not be afraid of an opponent second-guessing your play. Do not worry about being caught trying to steal. You cannot rely on receiving cards. You must be willing to both create and exploit opportunities. Take a chance on drawing hands early on if you can play cheaply. Be the first to go after uncontested pots. Mix up your play. Try some unorthodox maneuvers to keep your opponents from getting a read on you. Implement deception. The element of surprise is critical in warfare. This is how you disrupt your opponent's play. You want your opponent to doubt his own play. In tournament play when one mistake can mean elimination, the seed of doubt in your opponent provides you with a tremendous advantage. Players freeze rather than risk chips when they lack confidence. You do not just want to be a force. You want to be a disruptive force. That requires you to be unpredictable. Naked aggression is transparent. Strategic aggression is effective.

Enforce your rules. Raise opponents who limp in. Bet out when your opponent is vulnerable. Defend blinds and protect your stack. Do not chase drawing hands. Do not play when your opponent has the advantage. Defend and protect your assets.

If you consistently enforce your rules and create doubt in your opponents' play, you will be able to dictate the terms of play. Opponents will tighten up whenever you are in a pot. They will conform their play to yours. You will be able to outplay them at every turn. When they have strong hands, you will know it. However, those hands will be the only pots they win. You will win the uncontested pots. If an opponent challenges your rules, do not back down. Make him pay for it. There will be times when an opponent gets the best of you, but make him earn it when he does. Do not concede anything.

Stay abreast of the situation. Know the stakes. Be bold like a beast but have the intelligence of a general. Be a tactician. Things change quickly in tournaments. Your strategy must keep up. For example, a player you have been pushing around may now be short-stacked and in danger of elimination yet still have enough chips to do damage. This is now a dangerous opponent, and you must be careful how you play against him. If he is tournament savvy, he is likely to take a stand rather than be eliminated without a fight. You must take note of every change and watch how those changes are affecting everyone at the table.

Of course, the biggest change that can take place is a sizable difference in your own chip stack. In tournaments, you can go from a large stack to a small stack, or a small stack to a large stack, in one hand. If a change like this happens, take a deep breath and adjust. Do not get caught up in the moment. The swings in tournaments can be very emotional. It is imperative to stay objective and detached. Keep your emotions in check. Maintain the mind-set of a general. Observe the new landscape and adjust your tactics accordingly.

No matter how perilous or hopeless the situation looks, surrender is never an option. In tournaments, either you are eliminated or you win it all. Until then, you are engaged in a contest that requires your full attention and ability.

In tournaments, be prepared for anything. Stand ready to attack. Exercise virtu. Be a Prince. Adjust your strategy to keep up with the constant changes. Indulge your animal instincts. Be a tactician. Do those things you do not dare to do in your civilian life. Use position. Be proactive. Do not be afraid. Fortunately, this is not war. It is only poker. Have fun with it.

Glossary

All-in: To place all of one's chips in the pot. To go "all-in" is to bet your entire stack.

Ante: A set amount of chips that each player (including the blinds) must place in the pot before a hand is dealt. In No Limit Hold'em Tournaments, antes typically are not required until the later rounds.

Back door flush: Possessing three cards to a flush with only two more cards to come offers you a back door flush draw. If you happen to catch those two cards of the same suit that you need, you have made a back door flush.

Bad beat: Having a strong hand beaten by an opponent who was a big underdog but makes a lucky draw. This is especially true when your opponent has played poorly and should not have been in the pot in the first place.

Best of it: Having the best chance of winning the hand at that particular time.

Bet: To be the first to place chips in the pot on any given round.

Big blind: Typically, that position which is two spots to the left of the button. The big blind must lead the first round of betting with a forced full bet.

Blank: A card that does not help any player.

Blind: A forced bet that one or two players are forced to make to start the first round of betting. The blinds will be the first to act in each subsequent round of betting, and, thus, to be in the blind is to be in an unfavorable position. The blinds rotate around the table with each deal and are always to the left of the button.

Blinded out: To lose your chip stack because of posting (placing your chips in the pot) the mandatory blinds and antes.

Bluff: A bet or raise made to force your opponent to fold when you sense he is vulnerable, even though he may have a better hand.

Board: The five community cards placed in the center of the table.

Button: A round disk that rotates around the table with each new deal. The player on the button acts last during each round of betting, and thus, to be on the button is to be in the most favorable position.

Call: To place in the pot an amount of chips equal to an opponent's bet or raise.

Caller: A player who makes a call.

Calling station: A weak player who will call just about any bet but will rarely bet or raise. This type of player is extremely hard to bluff.

Chase: To stay in a hand with the hopes of outdrawing an opponent with a superior hand.

Check: To pass when it is your turn to bet.

Check-raise: To check and then raise after your opponent bets.

Chip: A round token used to represent varying denominations of money.

Covered: To have someone covered means you have more chips than he does.

Door card: The first card dealt face up to each player in seven card stud.

Draw (or on a draw): When you do not have a made hand but you hope to improve your hand by catching a few choice cards, you are on a draw.

Drawing dead: Holding a hand that cannot possibly win because no matter what card comes up, your opponent will still hold a superior hand.

Draw out: To improve your hand so that it beats a previously superior hand.

Early position: Any position in which you will act before most of the other players in a round of betting. In a ten-handed game, the first five positions to the left of the button will be considered early positions.

Favorite: A hand that has the best chance of winning at any point in time before all the cards are dealt.

Fifth Street: The fifth and final community card in hold'em or the sixth card dealt in seven card stud. Also called the river in hold'em.

Flop: The first three community cards, which are all dealt at the same time.

Flush: Five cards of the same suit.

Fold: To drop out of a hand rather than call a bet or raise.

Fourth Street: The fourth community card in hold'em or the fourth card dealt in seven card stud. Also called the turn in hold'em.

Free card: A card that a player gets to see without having to pay for it. When no one bets on a particular round of playing, the next card is considered a free card.

Full house: Three cards of one rank and two of another such as K♦, K♠, K♣, 3♠, 3♦.

Gut shot: An inside straight draw.

Half bet: In hold'em, the small blind is required to post a half bet.

Heads-up: To play against a single opponent.

Inside straight draw: A straight that can be completed only by a card of one rank. For example, 3, 4, 5, 7 can only be completed with an 8.

In the money: In tournament play, only the top finishers will receive prize money. A player who advances to receive prize money is said to have finished in the money.

Kicker: A side card that is not part of any made hand. For example, if you hold A, K and the board is A, Q, 4, 9, 9, you have a hand of two pair (Aces and nines) with a K kicker.

Late position: Any position in which you will act after most of the other players in a round of betting. In a ten-handed game, the button and the two positions to the right of the button will be considered late positions.

Lay down: To fold your hand in the face of a bet.

Levels: Predetermined intervals of play whereby the blinds (and antes, if applicable) will be set for a period. The blinds will increase with each level.

Limp(s) in: To call a bet rather than raise prior to the flop.

Loose: A player who is playing loose is playing more hands than he should.

Middle pair: To pair the second highest card on the board.

Middle position: A position in a round of betting somewhere in the middle. In a ten-handed game, the fourth and fifth positions to the right of the button are considered middle positions.

Muck: To discard a hand without revealing it.

Multiway pot: A pot with three or more players.

Nut flush draw: Drawing to the best possible flush hand. In hold'em, if you are holding A ♦, 4 ♦ and the board is Q ♦, 10 ♦, 4 ♣, one more diamond will give you the nut flush.

Nuts: The best possible hand at that point in time.

Off-suit: Two or more cards of different suits. If you are dealt a Jack of diamonds and the ten of spades, your hand is J, 10 off-suit.

On the bubble: In tournament play, when players are only a few eliminations away from being in the money. If a player is eliminated in twenty-eighth place when twenty-seven places were paid, that player is said to have been eliminated on the bubble.

On tilt: To be playing poorly due to a lack of control of your own play.

Outs: When you do not have the best hand, but there are still more cards to come; those cards that will make your hand a winning hand are called your *outs.*

Overcard(s): To have a card(s) that is higher than any card on the board. If you have K ♠, J ♦ and the flop is Q ♥, 4 ♣, 7 ♠, then you have one overcard.

Pair: Two cards of the same rank such as 6♣, 6♥.

Pocket: Your unexposed cards are called your pocket cards.

Pot: The collective amount of all chips bet at any point in time.

Pot odds: The ratio of the amount of chips in the pot to the size of the bet you must call.

Put your opponent on a hand: To determine to the best of your ability the hand your opponent is most likely to possess.

Rainbow: Two to four cards of different suits. If the flop comes 3, 6, J rainbow, then all three cards are of different suits.

Raise: To bet an additional amount after an opponent makes a bet.

Raiser: A player who makes a raise.

Rebuy: A rebuy tournament allows a player to rebuy chips for a predetermined amount of time and typically only if the player has less than the original buy-in amount. For example, if a rebuy tournament costs $100 to enter, and each player receives 1,000 in chips, players will be allowed to buy an additional 1,000 in chips for another $100 so long as they have less than 1,000 chips at the time of the rebuy. The rebuy option is usually only available for the first three levels of the tournament.

Ring game: A single table nontournament game of poker. Also called a side game.

River: The fifth and final community card in hold'em. Sometimes called fifth street. The seventh and final card in seven card stud.

Runner: A card that helps or completes your hand when you need help and that comes on the turn or river or both. For example, you are holding J♥,10♥ and the flop is J♠, A♥,2♦. Your opponent is holding A♦, J♣. Since no one card will help you, you need two runners in order to win. If the turn is 4♥ and the river is 9♥, you will have hit two runners and made a flush to win the hand.

Semi-bluff: To bet with the intention of inducing an opponent with a superior hand to fold, but if he does not, you have a reasonable chance to improve your hand to the best hand.

Set: In hold'em, three of a kind when you have a pocket pair and the board contains a card of the same rank.

Short-stacked: Playing with a stack of chips that is much smaller than the other players' average chip stack.

Showdown: The turning over of all remaining players' cards after the last round of betting is concluded.

Side Game: A single table nontournament game of poker. Also called a ring game.

5

Glossary

Sixth Street: The sixth card dealt in seven card stud.

Slow play: To not bet or raise with a strong hand in order to trap your opponent and, ultimately, win more chips in the hand.

Small blind: The first position which is immediately to the left of the button. The small blind typically must post a half bet before the cards are dealt.

Steal: To make a big bet or raise that induces your opponent(s) to fold when you may not have the best hand.

Straight: Five cards of mixed suits in sequence.

Suck out: To draw to a winning hand when the odds are greatly against it.

Suited: Two or more cards of the same suit.

Super satellite tournament: A tournament where the winner(s) gain entry into a higher entry fee tournament.

Tell: A nuance or mannerism a player may display that gives away his hand.

Tight: Playing very conservatively or only playing strong hands.

Underdog: A hand that is not the favorite to win.

Under the gun: The first player to act on the first round of betting in hold'em. Since the blinds have forced bets, the player to the immediate left of the big blind is *under the gun*.

Worst of it: Being an underdog to your opponent(s) at that point in time.

About the Author

David Apostolico has been playing poker for over twenty-five years. He has won tournaments in Las Vegas, Atlantic City and online and has finished in the money at the U.S. Poker Championships (Hold'em event). David plays poker on every level from home games to top tournaments with the best professionals in the world, including events on the Professional Poker Tour. David's previous book, *Tournament Poker and The Art of War* (Lyle Stuart, March 2005), incorporated the time-honored philosophies contained in Sun Tzu's classic *The Art of War* and applied them to poker tournaments. Like *Machiavellian Poker Strategy, Tournament Poker and The Art of War* helps poker players develop the proper attitude and mind-set to be successful at the poker table.

David received his J.D., with honors, from the University of North Carolina School of Law in 1988. Upon graduation, he went to work for the Wall Street law firm of Winthrop, Stimson, Putnam & Roberts where he spent a number of years specializing in mergers and acquisitions. During his legal career, David has found the principles he learned at the poker table to be enormously useful in his negotiations on behalf of clients large and small from multi-billion-dollar corporations to family businesses.

Currently, David lives with his family outside of Philadelphia, where he practices corporate law and plays competitive poker whenever he gets the opportunity.